TO THE DEVIL

WITH

OPERA

It's all about

Sex

Religion

Myths

Michael Kreps

First Published in 1998 by

Cardinal Press
9 Foreland Court
London
NW4 1LG

E-mail: Cardinal@London.7.demon.co.uk

© Michael Kreps

ISBN 0 9533505 0 9

A CIP record for this book is available from the British Library

Typeset in Times New Roman 11pt.

With appreciation to *Audrey White*, for her early encouragement and typing contribution before I learnt to process my own words. To my brother *Lionel* for his patience in reading, re-reading and commenting on never-ending variations of the same old thing. And most particularly to *Elisabeth Ingles*, for her constructive and encouraging critique and exposure of my worst errors of omission and commission, which I hope have been corrected.

Author's biographical note:

Michael Kreps is retired, and lives in NW London. He has 40 years' experience in never having written anything longer than a two-page document, usually for people who really only wanted to read one page, and he has had an even longer time to develop his interest in opera. These two elements have been fused to produce this book.

CONTENTS

PROLOGUE

PART 1:   THE JUDEO-CHRISTIAN GOD

PART 2:   GREEK MYTHOLOGY and LEGENDS

CONTENTS

PROLOGUE

Whenever I go to an opera, I leave my senses and reason at the door with my half-guinea and deliver myself up to my eyes and my ears.

Lord Chesterfield: 'Letters to his son', 23rd January 1752.

In vivo

You never get a second chance to make a first impression, and first impressions of opera are often the defining ones that stay throughout life. This first experience may come early or late; no matter, it's usually the one that counts and for me it came, so I was told, very early indeed. And although it has made a lifelong impression on me I don't remember a thing about it--which opera it was, the singers, the conductor--I know none of this; only where (at Covent Garden), and approximately when, it happened. For I was not yet born. My mother used to tell me from time to time, when I'd just again spent my last shillings on yet another opera record and would have to scrounge my week's lunch money from her, that my father had taken her to the opera when she was about six or seven months pregnant with me and she knew that I was enjoying the experience when, as soon as the overture started, I stopped kicking her and settled down, allowing us both to enjoy the evening.

Umbrellas

The great majority of all opera stories appear to spring from just three

1

sources: *Religion* (which includes both Judeo-Christian and pagan religions), *Myths and Legends* (both Greek and Nordic), and of course *Sex*, without which almost no opera is complete; most operas seem to contain at least two of these three elements. But since religion and sex have always been two of the most potent influences on human behaviour this is not surprising. It seems just a toss-up as to whether the myths or the Bible contain more tales of sex, rape, violence and murder. The Bible itself contains so much sexual violence and allusion that only the somewhat archaic language shelters its meanings from children who would otherwise surely find it on a parental list of banned books; for instance the biblical phrase 'lie with me' doesn't have the resonance of present-day 'let's go to bed and make love'; or 'he forced her' is not quite so explicit as 'he raped her'. These and similar expressions appear all through the Bible, and combine with descriptions of such violence, incest, murder, mass slaughter, and general mayhem as to provide ample cause to wonder about the private thoughts of those who originally compiled it.

There have been 'biblical' operas by the dozens. Most are drawn from the Old Testament, which seems reasonable since this comprises some 80% of the Bible and covers events spanning over three thousand years, whereas the New Testament covers only about 100 years and is essentially focused on the events of a single lifetime. But outside of the biblical operas Christianity has had a significant influence on the development of opera stories; for instance specifically Christian operatic themes have covered the conflict between God and the Devil, inter-religious prejudice and hatreds, stories about the Saints, and so on. And then there are the castrati, whose arrival can be directly traced back via Pope Gregory VI to St. Paul. But not every chapter here is about operas *per se,* and the castrati phenomenon was so significant (and interesting) that I have included it in a separate chapter on voice-types. Similarly there are chapters on the Devil, and on the Saints and how they have been brought to life in opera.

Even more significant numerically than the Judeo-Christian religions as a source of opera stories are the myths of earlier civilisations. The Greek stories for instance, usually starting from the plays and writings of those early literary giants Euripides, Sophocles, Aeschylus and Homer have inspired hundreds of operas; although, as with the biblical and "religious" operas, relatively few have survived. *Elektra, Ariadne auf Naxos, Orpheus and Eurydice, Médée* are among the better known. The Nordic myths, so magnificently brought to life by Wagner through his *Ring* cycle, are another source.

But of course opera is not opera without love, sex and seduction. Love can be featured without a primarily sexual component to it, in Beethoven's *Fidelio,* for instance, and usually between the hero and heroine. However, sex rears its ugly head when the villain (or whoever is cast as the bad guy) makes his appearance, since his interest in the girl is usually limited to her body. Right from the earliest days of opera sex has been a powerful idea when, way back in 1643, Monteverdi's *L'Incoronazione di Poppea* told how Poppea used her womanly charms to achieve her ambition in a totally male-dominated environment. Not a lot has changed, either in opera or real life, from Poppea's day. The opera genre is probably the only one that can rival the Bible and the legends for stories of sex and sexual violence, but even here seduction seems to have been a later development. For whilst both the

Greek/Nordic myths and the Bible are full of incidents detailing sexual desire and fulfilment (generally in the form of male lust followed by rape), the art or technique of seduction didn't seem to appear, operatically speaking, until much later, around the time of Mozart.

I have tried to take a look behind the (usually) well-known stories to see who, or what, was the story behind the story; to look more at the people, the places, the events that are featured in the operas. For instance, who was Samson? Was he any more than just a divinely inspired long-haired strongman who was brought down by sexual desire? What was the ingredient that da Ponte, who wrote those three great libretti for Mozart, shared with Beaumarchais, who wrote the original of one of them? Why does Babylon appear so often as an operatic location? Was the Dance of the Seven Veils anything more than just a stripper's routine? Who were those men and women, gods and goddesses who weave their way in and out of the "mythic" operas, and how do they connect with or relate to each other?

Structurally, each Part here deals with a number of operas grouped together under an umbrella; the treatment is to outline the *background* to the story, which may concern the principal character(s), the socio-political environment, the location, or whatever, then broadly sketch the story as it actually (or legendarily) happened, and then cover the opera itself. Sometimes the opera story so closely follows the original that a full treatment would be merely repetitious; where this is the case, it is indicated.

Part 1 has the Judeo-Christian umbrella. It covers biblical stories and operas on Samson, Moses, Herod and Salome, and others; crucifixion legends, the Inquisition, religious prejudice, stories of the Saints (and a big sinner), the synagogue cantors, and the Devil. Also included here is a chapter on voices, included in this part specifically because of the Christian influence on the castrati phenomenon; and there is a brief tongue-in-cheek review of Idolatry in opera.

Parts 2 and 3 have a Mythic umbrella and deal with the Greek and the Nordic legends respectively. The Trojan War was a prolific source of wonderful stories of heroes, gods, goddesses all inter-acting with each other in spectacular ways and producing some great operas; these dominate the entire Greek genre. In a similar way, the Nordic stories are dominated, operatically speaking, by Wagner, and his *Ring* cycle is the principal source here.

Part 4, on Sex and Seduction, is the third of my three great opera themes and here the stories are grouped under an umbrella held up by Aphrodite, the goddess of love. Mozart is *the* influence, but he is nobly supported by such lechers as his librettist da Ponte and that great character Beaumarchais, not to mention earlier ones like Don Juan and Casanova.

I conclude with an Epilogue reviewing the fate of women in opera; the losers, (i.e. those who end up dead, which means nearly all of them) in serious, or tragic opera , and the winners (i.e. those who get their man and, usually, his money), in comic opera. Why this should be, that comic opera heroines are more successful than their serious sisters, I don't know. But perhaps it has to do with it being *comic* opera!

PART 1. THE JUDEO-CHRISTIAN GOD

1.   MOSES, BABYLON AND THE OLD TESTAMENT

How odd of God to choose the Jews.
His son's a Jew; I thought you knew.

Anon

Moses

The first and greatest of the leaders of the Israelite people, Moses was, from his very first days, marked out as someone likely to be very special, except that at the time nobody seems to have noticed. The story is well-known of how his mother tried to save him from Pharaoh's attempt at statutory control of the Israelite numbers, which required that all Jewish male babies had to be consigned to the Nile river; she placed him in a reed basket and floated him down the river where he was found and adopted by, of all people, Pharaoh's daughter. Taking the advice of one of her maids, who turned out to be Moses' sister Miriam, the baby was placed with a Jewish woman to be suckled. Miriam was able to arrange that this should be his own mother. The first life-saving miracle had occurred.

A few years later, as a young boy in Pharaoh's court, Moses had the audacity to go up to Pharaoh, remove his crown and place it on his own head. To determine if this extraordinary and unheard-of action was just a small boy's innocent game or whether there might be some significance behind it, Pharaoh's wise men arranged a test; Moses was shown two bowls, one filled with scintillating precious stones and the other with glowing red-hot coals. He was told to pick from one of them and, not being silly, naturally reached out for the bowl with the precious stones.

6

However, the Archangel Gabriel was watching; he re-directed Moses' hand to the glowing coals and caused him to lift one to his mouth. This of course caused him to burn his tongue and lip, but also demonstrated to the court that he was after all just an ordinary silly boy and no significance was to be attached to the crown incident. The second life-saving miracle had now occurred. (This story does not appear in the Bible but is one of the Talmudic legends relating to the time, and at least has the merit of providing a possible explanation for the slow speech and stammer that afflicted Moses.)

Moses' next encounter with Divine forces was the drama of the Burning Bush where God, in person this time, appointed a very reluctant Moses to lead his people out of Egypt and assigned his more fluent brother Aaron to overcome Moses' protests about his speech problems. However, as he left home for Egypt with his wife Zipporah and their two sons, Moses' next encounter with God was almost his last, for Exodus records (4:24-26) that God intended to kill him because his first-born son had not been circumcised. Quickly Zipporah grabbed a sharp stone and performed the operation herself there and then, thus averting God's anger. From then on Moses was constantly guided and directed by God in his task of obtaining the release of the Israelites from Egypt and ensuring their survival in their subsequent wanderings.

His own later personal encounters with God on Mount Sinai mark Moses out as one of the truly special people not just of biblical but of all times, for he is the only person of whom it is said not simply that he met directly with God, but that God had shown himself. To Aaron and Miriam, God said that he spoke *mouth to mouth* with Moses (Numbers 12:8). Moses is credited with being the writer, under instruction from God, of the first five books of the Bible (The Pentateuch), with only the final verses of Deuteronomy, which describe the events leading to his

7

death, being written by his successor Joshua. As a leader, administrator of the task of keeping his people together throughout their 40-year wanderings through Sinai, as a lawgiver and judge, his life and achievements are sufficient to ensure his status as one of the greatest men in history. Operatically speaking, however, only the Burning Bush encounter with God, the Golden Calf episode, and the flight from Egypt have been featured.

The story of the Burning Bush has appeared in only one opera, Schoenberg's unfinished (he only completed two of an intended three acts) *Moses und Aaron* but the much greater human drama of the exodus from Egypt after Pharaoh had finally been cowed by the tenth plague is the subject of two works by Rossini; the first in 1818 as **Moses in Egypt**, and the revised version in 1827 as **Moses and Pharaoh: or, the crossing of the Red Sea**.

Modern archaeological scholarship has it that there never was a crossing of the Red Sea; the spectacular event described in the biblical account occurred, assuming that it did indeed happen, much further north in the northeast corner of Egypt by the Sea of *Reeds*. The first appearance of the *Red* Sea seems to have been in the 3rd century BCE Septuagint translation of the Bible.

EXODUS AND THE ROUTE OF THE WANDERING
EARLY 13TH CENTURY B.C.

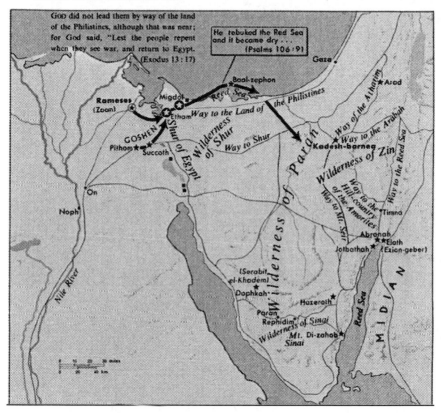

Reproduced with the kind permission of ©HarperCollins

The biblical narration records: 'And they took their journey from Succoth, and encamped in Etham,...' (Ex:13:20); in Ex.14:2 God instructed Moses to camp on the night before the crossing at 'Pi-Hahiroth, between Migdal and the Sea, over against Baal-Zephon'. It is also recorded (in Ex 14:9) that the pursuing Egyptians overtook the Israelites 'beside Pi-Hahiroth and before Baal-Zephon'. These places, Succoth, Etham, Migdal, and Baal-Zephon, have all been identified with possible sites near the Mediterranean end of the Gulf of Suez branch of the Red Sea (see the map 'Exodus and the route of the Wandering'). There are no suggested sites near to the 'traditional' Aqaba crossing point; whereas all those possible are in the location of the so-called Sea of Reeds, an area of large, shallow, reedy lakes, and thus it would appear to have been there that the fleeing Israelites were trapped. There is also the matter of the east wind to which the biblical account refers (Ex.14:21), for this would have been far more likely to have blown up by the Mediterranean than further south by Aqaba. The biblical miracle could of course have occurred at the Sea of Reeds just as easily as at the traditional Gulf of Aqaba crossing point, although biblical traditionalists point out that the Sea of Reeds location could not be right since it was simply not deep enough to have drowned the Egyptians. However a miracle is a miracle; it can occur anywhere and always overcomes mere reasoning. For me, the location of Baal-Zephon and the other sites places the event, miraculous or not, up by the Mediterranean and the Sea of Reeds, which is quite a long way from the Red Sea.

Following his later two meetings with God on Mount Sinai, and the destruction of the Golden Calf, Moses went on to lead his people through their long 40-year ordeal to the Promised Land; he was not however allowed by God to enter there himself, due to his own fit of temper years earlier which God regarded as a lack of faith. With the Promised Land in sight, Moses was instructed to climb Mount Nebo from where he would be able to see the new country, and was himself never seen again. He was then, by the biblical account, 120 years old.

'Moses in Egypt'   Rossini, 1818

God is using Moses as His agent to force Pharaoh to release the Israelites, the plagues being His instruments of pressure. The principal characters are Moses, his brother Aaron (re-named Eliezer in the later work), his sister Miriam, and Pharaoh; Rossini introduces Elcia as Miriam's daughter, and involves her in a clandestine love affair with Pharaoh's son, Osiride. Elcia is increasingly concerned about being parted from Osiride as Pharaoh's resolve is weakened by each new plague, and eventually she reveals that she and Osiride are in fact married. God resolves this problem for her when Osiride raises his sword in anger against Moses and is promptly struck down by a thunderbolt. The final scene in both works is the crossing of the Red Sea; this created such huge production difficulties in the original 1818 staging of the crossing, that Rossini was forced to re-write the entire scene, and in his revision added a prayer by Moses intended (stage-wise) to divert attention from the scene-shifting work going on. This new prayer 'Dal tuo stellato soglio...' ('from your star-girt throne...') was so moving and musically effective that it has become the best-known item in both versions. The Israelites, trapped between the pursuing Egyptians behind them and the impassable barrier of the Red Sea in front, begin to panic; however Moses calms them and commences, initially alone then joined by Aaron/Eliezer, Miriam and Elcia, a prayer for deliverance. The Red Sea parts, the Israelites cross, and the sea closes over the pursuing Egyptians.

Schoenberg wrote only two acts of a planned three-act work called **Moses und Aaron**, covering the period from Moses' sighting of the Burning Bush to the time of the Israelites' wanderings in the Sinai, and specifically including the period during which Moses was absent on the mountain receiving God's commandments whilst Aaron participated in the building and worship of the Golden Calf. (It is an interesting, though not original observation, that Moses brought down from the mountain ten simple rules carved on just two stone tablets to guide the future behaviour of the Israelites; thousands of years later these Ten Commandments still have universal application and receive universal respect, yet to adapt any one of them to our present civilisation requires the paper equivalent of a forest.)

Babylon and Nebuchadnezzar

Babylon's first biblical mention is in Genesis, the first book of the Old Testament, with the description of the construction of the Tower of Babel (Babylon's earlier name). Its final mention is in Revelation, the last book of the New Testament, with descriptions of the city as 'Babylon the Great, the Mother of Harlots' and its destruction. Between these two, Babylon features in many biblical stories as a great city, both in its heyday and in decline. There are numerous opera stories based on events in and around biblical Babylon, drawn from a number of the Old Testament books; for instance Genesis provides the **Tower of Babel**, a now forgotten work, the Book of Daniel the **Burning Fiery Furnace**, an event which occurred there; and also **Cyrus in Babylon.** The best known of all is of course Verdi's **Nabucco**.

12

Nebuchadnezzar, one of the greatest of the Babylonian rulers, was the famous and powerful king who completed the magnificent restoration of the city started by his father. He is said to have been responsible within this restoration programme for having constructed what became one of the wonders of the ancient world, the Hanging Gardens, reputedly built for the benefit of his homesick Medean Queen. He also gave the city wide streets and huge, thick, supposedly impregnable walls. But Nebuchadnezzar was more than a great builder; he was also a successful general who warred victoriously with many countries, and he proved himself a truly great king during his long reign. He was not however a modest man, boasting about his rebuilt city 'Is not this Babylon the Great, that I myself have built for the Royal House with the strength of my might and for the dignity of my majesty?' This proved to be a pretty shallow boast since only 23 years later, in the first year of the reign of King Belshazzar, the city fell overnight to an assault by the Medes and Persians led by the Persian King Cyrus. This event is the subject of Rossini's opera *Cyrus in Babylon, or The Downfall of Babylon* which includes the biblical story of the interpretation by Daniel of the mysterious hand writing 'mene, mene, tekel, upharsin' on the wall of the room where Belshazzar was feasting.

Rossini also set his *Semiramide* in Babylon. This once extremely popular opera has a basic historical inaccuracy in that Queen Semiramide's rule *preceded* that of Nebuchadnezzar by a few hundred years, yet she has an early scene with Arsace which supposedly takes place in the Hanging Gardens, i.e. *before* they were constructed by Nebuchadnezzar. Rossini, presumably following his usual practice, decided to subordinate history to theatricality.

Semiramis

Semiramis (meaning 'the goddess is exalted') was the great Assyrian Queen who according to some legends was the daughter of the goddess Atagatis (also known as Astarte, or Ishtar, in other parts of the region). Her beauty had so captivated King Ninus, the founder of the Assyrian Empire, that he made her his queen. On Ninus' death she assumed power and reigned for many years, during which time she built Babylon and expanded the empire by conquests. The combination of her great achievements and outstanding beauty gave rise to the legends first of her birth, and later that after her death she became a dove. However there were also stories that Ninus' death was no accident but could be attributed to her. Voltaire's tragedy "Semiramis" is based on events in her life, as is Rossini's opera, which accepts the theory that she murdered her husband to gain power.

"Semiramide"   Rossini, 1823

Act 1 At the Temple of Baal in ancient Babylon, Queen Semiramide is expected to announce the name of the man who will succeed, 15 years after the death of her husband King Nino, to his throne. Assur, her ex-lover and accomplice in the murder of Nino, confidently expects to be named. The Queen however has come to love Arsace, the young commander of her army, and erroneously believes that he loves her. As Arsace arrives, she names him as king and as her new consort. Nino's ghost appears and calls upon Arsace to avenge his death by killing his murderers. Scene 2 of this Act, placed in The Hanging Gardens, contains some of Rossini's most beautiful music.

Act 2 Assur is furious at being passed over and threatens to reveal Semiramide's part in the murder if he is not made king; she in turn threatens to expose his complicity. Meanwhile the High Priest Oroe reveals to Arsace that he is actually the son of Nino and Semiramide, and that his mother was joined by Assur in Nino's murder. Arsace tells his mother what he knows; the marriage is now of course impossible. Assur vows to kill Arsace and they start to duel by Nino's tomb; Semiramide tries to stop them and is unintentionally killed by a blow from Arsace intended for Assur. Assur is arrested, Nino is avenged, and Arsace accepts the throne.

Nebuchadnezzar

Among his many conquests Nebuchadnezzar made two assaults on Jerusalem; from the first he took many prisoners and much booty, deposed the king and placed Zedekiah on his uncle's throne. The second was ten years later in 586 BC when he returned, sacked the city and destroyed the Temple as a reprisal for Zedekiah's rebellion, returning with more prisoners. Some two years later, Nebuchadnezzar had a strange dream, which he demanded of his wise men and soothsayers that they interpret for him even though he refused to tell them what it was that he had dreamed. It was then that Daniel appeared and first accurately described and then interpreted the dream; Nebuchadnezzar was so impressed that he heaped rewards on Daniel, also appointing his friends Shadrach, Meshach and Abednego to high positions. It was these friends (always appearing as a threesome) who were later sentenced to a spell in a burning fiery furnace for refusing to bow down to a great image Nebuchadnezzar had constructed; to everyone's astonishment, not least that of Nebuchadnezzar, the three emerged from the furnace unharmed. The king then became a believer in God. This story became the subject of an opera (a Church parable really, but included as an opera in all the dictionaries) by Benjamin Britten *"The Burning Fiery Furnace"*, and the whole episode and opera is wittily summarised in the following verses (by Ron Rubin, in *How to Be Tremendously Tuned in to Opera)*:

> In Babylon, three captive Jews
> At a feast, say, "O King we refuse
> To join in the gaiety,
> And worship your deity ---
> It's one of our basic taboos!"

> The King says "How dashed indiscreet ---
> You shall die in a fire of great heat!"
> When he sees they're unhurt,
> He cries: "Strewth, I'll convert!
> Please send for a rabbi, tout de suite!"

Later Nebuchadnezzar went mad, only recovering his sanity after several years, and then re-affirmed his belief in Daniel's God. Babylon did not long survive these events. After Cyrus captured the city, one of his successors, King Darius, destroyed the huge walls after a futile Babylonian revolt, and the city then steadily declined in importance. Alexander the Great later captured the city and, recognising its potential, ordered a rebuilding programme; however he died, in Nebuchadnezzar's former palace, before much work could be done.

"Nabucco" — Verdi, 1842

Originally Verdi had titled the opera *Nabucodonosor* but this was later reduced to and is now universally known as **Nabucco**. The opera covers the period from Nebuchadnezzar's second assault on Jerusalem and his destruction of Solomon's Temple, to his later madness and recovery, reassigning both the cause and duration of this madness. Aside from Nebuchadnezzar, the only other biblical character is Zechariah the

Prophet, who is portrayed as Zaccaria, the High Priest of the Hebrews. Zedekiah, King of Judah at the time, appears but only by reference as the King of Jerusalem and uncle to Ishmael; Ishmael is in love with Fenena, Nabucco's younger (and favourite) daughter, who returns his love. The other principal character is Abigail, Nabucco's elder (warrior) daughter, who also loves Ishmael.

The opera was a sell-out success from its opening and has continued to be one of the world's favourites. Verdi himself wrote that, dispirited by the failure of his first opera, he was reluctant to undertake another work but was persuaded to at least look at the libretto of a new work. Flicking through the pages his eyes followed the verses of what we now know as 'va pensiero', the hugely popular chorus of the Hebrew slaves, and he found himself mentally composing what became, and remains to this day one of the most famous and beautiful choruses in all opera. "I read through the verses (of 'va pensiero') and was deeply moved since they were almost a paraphrase of the Bible, which I have always enjoyed reading". The opening lines of the verse adapt Psalm 137 v.1-3, and immediately following this chorus Zaccaria makes the prophecy concerning Babylon that is in the Bible in Jeremiah 25:12. The opera is in four parts, each having a title and each being sign-posted by a reference/quotation from Jeremiah.

Part 1 - *Jerusalem* 'Thus saith the Lord: Behold I shall deliver this city into the hand of the King of Babylon, and he will burn it with fire.'

Nabucco's final assault on the city has succeeded; he is about to defile the Temple by riding into it on his horse, when he is stopped by Zaccaria who grabs Fenena and, holding a dagger to her, swears to kill her if Nabucco continues. He dismounts to consider the situation. Abigail, who deeply resents her sister, hopes that Fenena will indeed be killed, whilst Fenena begs her father to have pity. Nabucco, to gain time, reminds Zaccaria that he, Nabucco, has just defeated the God of the Jews in battle and that their God is therefore unlikely to intervene now. Ishmael however rescues Fenena from Zaccaria and, by freeing her, effectively delivers the city and the lives and freedom of his own people finally into Nabucco's hands.

Part 2 - *The Wicked Man.* 'Behold the whirlwind of the Lord goeth forth; it shall fall upon the head of the wicked.'

Now back in Babylon, Abigail has found a paper showing that she was born a slave and was adopted by Nabucco who intends, whilst he is away in Judea, for Fenena to rule in his name. Abigail plots with the Priests of Baal to seize the throne by putting out that Nabucco has been killed in battle. Nabucco, however, arrives back in the midst of a dispute between Abigail and Fenena over who shall wear his crown; he takes it, places it on his own head and challenges Abigail to take it from him. She is not yet prepared to do this.

Then he overreaches himself. He calls upon the assembled Priests, Hebrews and others to heed his words: first he disclaims the Babylonian god Baal, whom he accuses of complicity through the Priests in the plot to steal his crown, then he tells the Hebrews that their God, having been defeated in battle, clearly has no further influence, and finally he proclaims that there is demonstrably only one God, himself. He orders the assembled crowd to kneel, faces to the ground, and worship him: no longer king, but now God. There is a crash of thunder, and a thunderbolt cracks over Nabucco's head. The crown lifts from his head and crashes to the ground. His terror and dawning madness are obvious to everyone. He collapses. Abigail picks up the fallen crown.

Part 3 - *The Prophecy.* 'the wild beasts of the desert shall dwell in Babylon, and the owls shall dwell therein.'

Abigail now rules as de-facto Queen; the Priests suggest that Fenena, who has openly admitted that she has converted to Judaism, should be put to death with the rest of the Hebrews and Abigail readily agrees. She takes the death warrant to her father and easily tricks him into signing it; only then does she tell him that Fenena's name is included. He begs and pleads with her for Fenena's life but she merely scorns and insults him.

Scene 2 opens by the banks of the Euphrates with the Hebrews, in chains, singing the famous 'Va pensiero' chorus, of their longing for their own land:

'Fly thoughts, on wings of gold; go settle upon the slopes and hills where, soft and mild, the sweet airs of our native land smell fragrant'

Zaccaria appears and berates them with a fearsome prophecy:

'Rise up, brothers in anguish.
The Lord speaks from my lips.
In the obscurity of the future, I see.
Behold the shameful chains are broken!
The Wrath of the Lion of Judah already
falls upon the treacherous sand, to
settle upon the skulls, upon the bones.
Hither come the hyenas and the snakes:
midst the dust raised by the wind a
doomed silence shall reign!
The owl will spread abroad the sad lament
when evening falls. Not a stone will be
left to tell the stranger where once proud Babylon stood.'

Part 4 - *The Broken Idol.* "Baal is confounded, his idols are broken in pieces."

Nabucco hears voices outside the palace calling "death to Fenena" but he is helpless, locked in his room and in his madness. He stares out of the window into the street and in his despair he cries out to the God of the Hebrews for forgiveness and the restoration of his sanity, promising to rebuild the altar and the Temple, and to recognise the one true God. His mind immediately starts clearing; he realises that his repentance is accepted and that he is returning to normality. As Fenena and others are preparing for death there are sounds of "Long live Nabucco". He enters running, sword in hand, followed by loyal troops. He calls out to his men to break the idol of Baal, but it falls by itself and shatters. He turns to the Hebrews and tells them that they are free to return home and he exhorts them to rebuild the Temple. Abigail enters needing support, and begging the God of Israel to be forgiven. She collapses and dies.

Samson

The Book of Judges gives **Samson's** story which was re-told by Saint-Saëns in his 1877 work **Samson and Delilah**. Given the opera's title, it is not unreasonable to find that it completely ignores Samson's early life, and even what might have made a good opening scene, the visit to his hitherto childless mother by an Angel. She hears the message that:

> 'Thou art barren, and bearest not; but thou shalt conceive and bear
> a son. Now therefore beware; drink not wine nor strong drink,
> and eat not any unclean thing: For thou shalt conceive and bear a
> son; and no razor shall come upon his head: for the child shall
> become a Nazirite unto God from the womb: and he shall begin to
> deliver Israel out of the hands of the Philistines'
>
> (Judges 13:3-5).

Having discussed this visitation with her husband, who then asked to hear this same message for himself, the Angel reappeared and repeated his promise and requirements. Being thus satisfied, Samson's future father continued to do his marital duty by his wife so that in due course a son was indeed born whom they called Samson and who is one of only three Nazirites who are featured in opera (Samuel, and John the Baptist are the others). Nazirites should not be confused with Nazarenes (people of Nazareth); Nazirites were people who were singled out and dedicated either by divine process, as with Samson, or sometimes by self-dedication, for special service to God. One could thus volunteer to become a Nazirite for a specified period or even a lifetime; or like Samson be divinely appointed for life. There is a fine distinction to be drawn between, for example, Samson's and Samuel's Nazirite dedications, for Samuel's also barren mother prayed for a child, promising to dedicate it to the Lord if she were blessed in this way; whereas Samson's mother was visited, without previous prayer on her part, by an Angel with God's message concerning her as yet unconceived son, indicating his mission in life.

Thus Samson was sent deliberately and directly by God to fulfil a specific purpose, to deliver Israel out of the hands of the Philistines, and he might have been expected therefore to have been a well-nigh perfect tool for the job. Instead he proved to be badly flawed. Nazirites had not only to live a clean, wholesome and religiously observant life but were also required to follow three major rules. A Nazirite was not allowed to drink alcohol (hence the prohibition on Samson's mother concerning strong drink); nor to touch a dead body; nor to shave his hair ('no razor shall come upon his head'). Samson was simply not a very good Nazirite despite his divine appointment; he visited prostitutes (the one in Gaza, as well as Delilah), so obviously he didn't live a clean life. But more significantly he also broke all three major interdictions of his calling for he scooped honey with his bare hands from the insides of the corpse of the lion he had killed (also bare handed); he held and attended banquets lasting several days ('for so used the young men to do'), and of course in the end he allowed Delilah to give him a haircut.

When he grew up Samson married a non-Jewish woman, against the wishes of his parents: 'Is there not among the daughters of your brothers and among all my people a woman, so that you are going to take a wife from the uncircumcised Philistines?' And even though there was no prohibition about this, it doesn't seem the sort of action expected of a Nazirite, divinely appointed or not. After his wife betrayed him over the answer to a riddle he had set at a 7-day party he threw, he took her back to her father who gave her to someone else and then tried, in vain, to interest Samson in another of his daughters. Later Samson visited a prostitute in Gaza, and then fell for Delilah. Which is about where Saint-Saëns starts his opera.

"Samson and Delilah"   Saint-Saëns, 1877

This is the operatic version of Judges:16, with considerable licence. It could reasonably be sub-titled 'A Woman Scorned' in its treatment of Delilah's motives for ensnaring Samson. In the Bible story she is bribed and accepts money (1100 pieces of silver) for her part in Samson's downfall; but in Saint-Saëns' opera she refuses any bribes. She just wants to get her own back. Yet for all her significance in the Samson story, Delilah is in every other sense a woman of no importance; she just appears in the biblical story and then, having played her part, simply disappears, never to be heard of again. Her insight into, and understanding of, Samson were such however that she knew he was finally telling her the truth about his extraordinary strength when he prefaced his secret by saying 'I have been a Nazirite unto God...'; she knew he would never take the name of the Lord in vain.

When the opera opens the Hebrew's revolt against the Philistines has not yet begun (and Samson's biblical feats of arms with the lion and with the ass's jawbone are not referred to). He has clearly enjoyed an intimate relationship previously with Delilah, and her reason for plotting his downfall is simply that of personal revenge because he left her before she was ready to let him go, so offending her pride. Delilah's motivation is thus to humiliate Samson and, totally confident that he is still in sexual thrall to her, she intends to use the power this gives her for her own ends. As well as her entrance number in the Temple dance, Delilah is given two beautiful arias in her campaign to re-conquer Samson. The second, the very well-known 'My heart opens to your voice' is the most famous song in the opera; coming from the throat of the right woman it could bring to his knees a man of steel, whilst Samson, even with his God-given strength, was still only flesh and blood. For me (also mere flesh and blood), the right throat would the one owned by the great Russian mezzo Elena Obraztsova; she could give me a haircut anytime.

Act 1 The opening scene provides a non-biblical opportunity for Samson to instigate the uprising by killing a senior Philistine official. He then leads the Hebrews' escape into rebellion, causing the High Priest, who appears too late to see anything but the dead body, to prophetically curse Samson: 'May a worthless woman finally betray his love. Forever accursed be the Children of Israel! ... Accursed be he who leads them!'

Sometime later in the same Temple Square, Delilah and the priestesses emerge from the Temple. Delilah greets Samson with honeyed words that tell of her continuing love for him. Samson knows his weakness for this woman and prays for strength to resist her. Delilah joins with the priestesses in a voluptuous dance, aware that Samson is unable to resist following her with his eyes. She then sings her first great aria, 'Spring that returns...'

Act 2 opens with Delilah musing on the progress of her campaign to entrap Samson. Her feminine instincts tell her that Samson will not be able to resist visiting her that evening, and that she will then be able to gain her revenge. The High Priest arrives to enlist her aid in overcoming Samson, promising to pay any price she asks for her successful support. Delilah however scorns the offer, confessing that she hates Samson as much as does the High Priest, that three times she has tried, unsuccessfully, to discover the secret of his strength. But now, she knows she will win; he will come to see her tonight, and will be unable to resist her tears.

In the evening Samson does indeed arrive, intending, as he tells Delilah, to end the relationship since he cannot serve God and also be with her. Delilah produces her tears, and with devastating effect. Samson simply cannot resist her and passionately declares his love, which is so great that he will defy God Himself for her.

Delilah responds by singing her second great aria and gets around to what she really wants, the secret of his strength. After all, she says, you can trust me! (She sounds like a politician.) She pleads for his secret, but Samson resists. A storm rages overhead, with thunder and lightning. Frustrated at his unexpected resistance, Delilah decides to turn on the tears again, but Samson still refuses this final betrayal, knowing that the rolls of thunder overhead are God's way of indicating His displeasure. Delilah is getting nowhere, so she makes her last throw; calling him a stonehearted coward whom she despises, she turns and runs back to her dwelling. Samson gazes after her and in desperation, raising his arms to heaven in a gesture of his despair, rushes after her and follows her into the house. Soon afterwards, Delilah appears at a window and calls the hidden Philistine soldiers.

Act 3 In the final Act the blinded and shorn Samson has been taken to the Temple of Dagon to be mocked. Delilah achieves his final humiliation by telling him there that she had sold his secret in advance, and boasts that she has avenged her god, her people and herself. Pleading with God for one last chance to avenge Him, Samson has himself placed between the two central pillars of the temple. Then, with a final prayer (that closely follows Judges 16:28) to God for help, in one final surge of strength he leans on and shatters the pillars, bringing down the whole temple structure.

David

The Book of Samuel introduces **David**, who was one of the most interesting of all the Old Testament characters. I find it surprising that he has featured so little in opera; there are only four works noted; Milhaud wrote *David* (1954), to celebrate the 3000th anniversary of Jerusalem, Sutor (1812) and Galli (1904) both wrote operas which have not survived, and Nielsen wrote *Saul and David* (1902) which is reviewed below. David was a shepherd, songwriter and musician, poet, soldier, statesman, prophet and king; he was a man who excelled in all these fields yet who was also able to relate easily to the people whose leader he became. As befits such a man of parts he was also one who was much in need of women; he had eight wives, many concubines, and fathered over twenty children. He was not above using his position to seduce the wife of one of his people and then arrange for her husband to be sent to a war zone where he would quickly be killed. These sexual mores were inherited by a couple of his children; one son raped his half-sister (and was killed in revenge by her full brother), another usurped his father's property rights in his concubines, and then later tried to usurp his father's throne. David's career really took off when he became famous for having thrown a stone at Goliath; he was a friend of King Saul's son Jonathan, and by killing Goliath he gained first the respect and then the fear of Saul. It is this early period of David's life that is covered in Nielsen's opera.

"Saul and David"   Nielsen, 1902

In at least one respect this may be thought of as the most 'biblical' of all the operas, in that all the characters are drawn from the Old Testament story. Neither Nielsen nor his librettist Christiansen seemed to feel it necessary to introduce additional characters to fill out the action, presumably since everything was already there: the young shepherd David, from a humble background, who nevertheless wins the love of Michal, daughter of the revered and powerful King Saul; this same David who, in single combat, slays the terrifying giant Goliath; David's close friendship with Jonathan, one of Saul's sons and brother of Michal; Saul's fall from grace; Jonathan's death in battle; the downfall of Saul, and David's succession as King. There is more than enough in these events to provide all the drama and romance necessary, without introducing any other characters. Yet even the minor ones (Abner, one of Saul's officers, and David's friend Abisa) are in the bible story. There is even the Witch of Endor, otherwise recognisable as the biblical 'mistress of spirits' whom Saul consulted at her base in Endor. And of course there is the Prophet Samuel.

The time-scale of the opera is collapsed both to allow the events to be seen more easily in context and of course to be able to cover the major events within an evening's entertainment. Thus Goliath is not allowed forty days during which to taunt and terrify the Israelites; David despatches him soon after he appears. Much detail is also necessarily omitted in order to keep the work within reasonable bounds. So although in the opera Saul promises Michal to David if he kills Goliath, and then refuses to keep his promise, there is no reference to his later (biblical) agreement that David could marry her provided he presented Saul with the foreskins of 100 Philistines, even though the valiant David then doubled this to 200; the whole episode is omitted. (Given the nature of this price demanded by Saul for his daughter this is understandable; the staging difficulties might be awkward! But what on earth could have been in the minds of those who compiled the Bible, to have selected this one out of what must have been very many episodes available?) Again, in the Bible story David is thrown out by Saul who then marries off Michal to someone else whilst David consoles himself with other women; operatically however David and Michal are cast out together and thereafter stay together.

2.   SEVEN VEILS

The story of the beheading of John the Baptist is told in their Gospels by both Matthew and Mark, albeit with some differences of detail. It is almost the only New Testament event to have been given operatic treatment that has survived, and this has been done twice; first by Massenet, in **Herodias** and then some 23 years later by Richard Strauss with **Salome.** Both operas had to go through the censorship hoops before achieving production.

Salome

Based on Oscar Wilde's play of the same name, both the music and libretto of this opera were controversial; but used in the re-telling of a New Testament episode the work attracted even greater attention than the composer's name and reputation might have justified, and its reception around the world was as controversial as the work itself. At its debut performance in Dresden, it received 38 curtain calls; yet the Court Opera in Vienna refused to allow it to be presented there. In Berlin there were over 50 performances in its first two years. In New York, where its first production was in 1907, there was such a furore that it was withdrawn after the initial performance, and was not seen again there until 1933. In London the Lord Chamberlain banned it, which meant that no public performances were permitted although private ones were possible, and one of these was attended by King Edward VII. According to Artur Rubinstein (who was providing a piano accompaniment) the King thought there was nothing particularly shocking in it and did not understand the censor's objections to it.

The London problem, as recorded by Sir Thomas Beecham, who wanted to present it, was the Lord Chamberlain's difficulty concerning the representation on the stage of John the Baptist, a real biblical character.

Beecham pointed out that *Samson and Delilah* had been permitted several years earlier, and they were also real biblical characters. "There is a very great difference, Sir Thomas; in one case it is the Old Testament, and in the other it is the New." Clearly, whilst all parts of the Bible are holy, some parts are more holy than others!

Possibly the best-known stage aspect of *Salome* is the Dance of the Seven Veils, which is sometimes performed as if it were just a kind of striptease act. Yet the Dance of the Seven Veils has its origin as an important religious ritual. Ishtar, the Queen of Heaven in both ancient Babylonian and Hebraic (Jeremiah 44:17-19) theologies, is desperate to rescue her son Tammuz, who has been fatally wounded and is now in the Underworld. She prepares herself for her journey there dressed in her finest clothes, and at each of the seven stages of her descent to the Underworld she removes some of them, finally arriving completely nude and defenceless to plead for the return of Tammuz. This epic rescue journey by the goddess was celebrated as an annual temple ritual by her priestesses, the descent and disrobing being represented by the removal, one by one, of each of seven veils. The priestess enacting this ritual uses the name Salome (from the Hebrew word *shalom*, meaning *peace*) and, as with the original journey, when the final veil is removed she displays herself quite naked. By the time of Herod this ritual had become degraded to a mere entertainment.

The New Testament scriptures do not mention Salome by name, referring to her simply as the daughter of Herodias; nor is there any reference to the style of dance she performed. These details were given later by Flavius Josephus, the soldier/statesman/scholar of sometimes doubtful credentials who was born soon after these events. Josephus also offers some intriguing information concerning Salome, her mother Herodias and their marital choices. The Herodian dynasty (see the diagram

'Keeping it in the Family') was effectively consolidated by the man who became known as Herod the Great, a man who married ten times. Each wife provided him with both children and trouble, since they were always plotting to ensure the best futures for their own offspring. Indications of the extent of these troubles were that Herod executed three of his sons for plotting against him, and that he changed his will several times as the influence of his successive wives and their children waxed and waned.

One son, Philip, married Herodias who was the grand-daughter of Herod the Great's sister Salome, and thus his cousin; after Philip's death Herodias married his half-brother Antipas, the Herod of the biblical story, so arousing the fury of John the Baptist, who regarded this as an incestuous act. Herodias' daughter by her first husband Philip is the Salome featured in this opera and was thus Antipas' niece (through her father), and through her mother's re-marriage became his step-daughter also. Herodias clearly believed in keeping marriage in the family but in this she was merely following the Herodian family practice, as the family-tree demonstrates. Her brother Agrippa had a son and daughter by his marriage to a descendant of Herod the Great's brother Phasael, and these two took the "keep-it-in-the-family" approach a step further by indulging in an incestuous relationship of their own. Josephus later provides the information that after the Baptist beheading, Salome herself married an uncle, Philip of Iturea, another of Herod the Great's offspring (he had plenty, after all, even after executing three of them), and a half-brother of Herod Antipas. Following Philip's death, Josephus says that she then married her cousin Aristobulus, having three sons by him. Like her mother and other relatives, Salome obviously shared the view that marriage should be a family affair.

KEEPING IT IN THE FAMILY
or
The Marriage Lines of the Herods

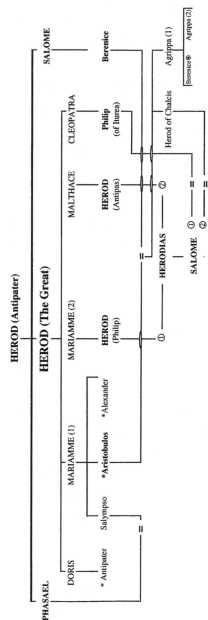

Notes:

1. Only the more interesting of the Herod family marriages are shown.
2. Only some of the more interesting, or significant of Herod the Great's marriages are shown
3. Herodias was the grand-daughter of Herod the Great by both of her parents, who were 1st cousins. She married two of her uncles.
4. Phasael married his niece Salympso.
5. Herod (of Chalcis) married his 1st cousin. Salome married a great-uncle.
6. = Indicates marriage.
7. ⊚ Sibling incest - Berenice/Agrippa.
8. * Executed by their father.

The Agrippa/Berenice incest probably did not disturb the family at the time as much it might do us, for this kind of relationship was not uncommon in royal circles in the region. The Ptolemy dynasty of Egypt practised brother/sister incest down the generations from the days of the very first Ptolemy. His mistress Thais had previously been mistress of Ptolemy's leader, Alexander the Great, until his untimely death; Ptolemy was extremely fond of her and she had three children by him, but it was his half-sister Berenice, his third wife, whose son became his heir and successor Ptolemy II. The practice of sibling incest was followed by the later Ptolemys; one, Ptolemy IX, even divorcing one sister in order to marry another. This could work two ways: Cleopatra (not the famous one, Cleopatra was even more common a name among the Ptolemys than was Salome among the Herods), the widow of Ptolemy VI who was also her late brother, married another brother who became Ptolemy VIII --- though not until he had killed his nephew Ptolemy VII, Cleopatra's son by her late brother and first husband Ptolemy VI. The supposed benefit of this sibling incest practice was to avoid dynastic squabbles (and worse) over inheritance!

For such a bit-player in history, however, Salome certainly seems to have managed to be at some significant places at the right time. In Mark's Gospel, there is a Salome reported as having been present at the Crucifixion (15:40), as having accompanied Christ in Galilee (15:41), and then (16:1) there is Salome present at the burial. Of course Salome was not an uncommon name in those times and there is no real evidence concerning who this Salome was; however, Robert Graves in the *White Goddess* deduces that she was the Salome who was Herodias' daughter.

Performing the Dance of the Seven Veils raised problems. The first Salome, at the Dresden premiere, initially refused the dance directions of the producer in rehearsals. 'I won't do it. I'm a decent woman'.

However, she did. Even today there is a prurient interest in this, not so much in the dance itself as in how much flesh will be revealed. And the music, with its modernist (in 1905) discords, upset many critics, including the composer's father who called it 'perverted' and described it as 'like having countless beetles crawling around inside your breeches'. Then, there was the libretto. Passions were expressed passionately, and lust was on offer for all to hear (and see):

> 'I am a man of middle life who has devoted upwards of 20 years to the practice of a profession that necessitated a daily intimacy with degenerates. I say after deliberation that Salome is a detailed and explicit exposition of the most horrible, disgusting, revolting and unmentionable factors of degeneracy that I have ever heard, read of or imagined'.
>
> (From a letter to the New York Times following the Salome performance)

In the Gospels' story Herod is accused by John the Baptist of incest for marrying Herodias, his late brother's wife. Herodias demanded John's imprisonment and execution, but Herod, whilst having John arrested and imprisoned, refused to execute him. It is at this point that Strauss's opera begins. It is Herod's birthday party, and John is in prison:

"Salome"   Richard Strauss, 1905

In this one-act work, Salome (because the original libretto, based on Oscar Wilde's original play was in French the name is often spelt with an acute accent over the 'e'; in German and English of course this is not required), Herodias' daughter by her first marriage and thus Herod's niece as well as his step-daughter, is a beautiful and sensual young woman. She leaves the banqueting hall, where Herod's party is in full flow, for the terrace to avoid the lecherous looks she's getting from Herod. Outside, she hears the voice of John (called Jokanaan in this work), calling from his cell below that the Son of Man has arrived, and becomes very curious about him. She persuades/seduces the Captain of the Guard into disobeying Herod's strictest orders and bringing the prisoner up from his cell so that she can see him. John appears and immediately fulminates in graphic language against the abominator inhabiting a bed of incestuousness. Salome is aware of course that John is referring to her mother but she is fascinated by him and tells him she is Herodias' daughter. His response is to reject her presence and to continue to express his opinions of her mother. Salome makes verbal love to John but he is disgusted by her and can only become free of her by returning to his cell.

Herod and Herodias go outside to the terrace. The restless Herod is looking for Salome and has to be warned by Herodias about his unhealthy interest in the girl; finding her, Herod asks her to dance for him but she refuses. Not until he promises to reward her with anything she wants does she suddenly become interested, and extracts from Herod his publicly sworn oath on this. She then performs the Dance of the Seven Veils and, after a brief discussion with her mother, appals Herod by asking as her reward for John's head, served to her on a platter. He protests vehemently but Herodias, who did not want her daughter to dance in the first place, now applauds the demand. Herod begs Salome to ask for something else; half the kingdom, the largest emerald in the world, his collection of white peacocks, anything but not John's head. The man comes from God, he says, he is a holy man touched by angels. But nothing, not offers of great wealth, huge possessions, can turn Salome. She wants John's head, and Herod is too weak to deny his public promise to her. Give her what she wants, he orders.

The executioner shortly appears, with John's head on a silver shield. Salome takes it and then in the opera's longest solo croons to it in the terms of the love talk she had spoken to John a little earlier. Finally, almost gloating that he'd refused to allow her to kiss him in life, she leans over the bloody head and kisses its mouth. Herod is disgusted but then seeing her again kissing the head is suddenly revolted and appalled. 'Kill that woman!' he calls out to his guards. They advance on her and crush her beneath their shields.

Hérodias, Massenet's 1881 work, is an earlier and much less sensational telling of the Salome story. Herodias, in this version, is unaware that Salome is her long-lost daughter; rather, she sees Salome, the target of much attention from Herod, as her rival. Salome admits to being in love with John so Herod, angry at her refusal of his offers, orders the arrest and execution of both Salome and John. In prison they declare their mutual love. Salome blames Herodias for her fate and would like to have her killed. There is no dance, and no execution of John in this opera, which does not really have a chance now against the Strauss version.

3.   HOW TO LOSE ONE'S HEAD OVER A WOMAN.

Two good Apocryphal tales for opera both focus on a woman. *Judith,* who raised the siege of her home town of Bethulia by killing the besieging army's General; and Susanna who was the victim of entrapment by two elders from her community. Judith's story has been written about a number of times, but only one version has had any success. *Susannah* was very effectively transferred from its biblical time and location to a Tennessee valley in the mid-20th century, and from the Jewish community to an isolated Christian community. Although well-received at its original production in 1955, it has not had many airings in recent years.

"Judith"   Serov, 1863

The Apocrypha of Judith tells in very considerable detail of a siege by Holofernes, who was Nebuchadnezzar's general. It appears from the events re-told that this was not the biblical Nebuchadnezzar (*Nabucco,* of operatic fame) but a later, some 70 years later, king of the same name.

The Apocrypha story tells how Holofernes was besieging the small walled Jewish town of Bethulia. He called a council of officers and was advised by one, Achior, that the Jews could only be conquered if they had offended their God. "Leave them alone" was his advice. Holofernes rejected this and took control of the town's water supplies which were at the foot of the hills outside; by simply depriving the citizens of their water, he planned to avoid having to fight a battle. After 34 days of siege, the Jews agreed among themselves that they could only hold out for another 5 days; if no help came in that time they would have to surrender.

Living in Bethulia was Judith, the still very attractive, albeit retired widow of a wealthy merchant. Hearing of this surrender plan, she went to the city's leaders, gave them a large piece of her mind over their lack of faith in God, and promised that she herself, with God's help, would raise the siege. After prayer, she dressed herself up in her finest clothes and, taking a supply of kosher food and drink, she and her maid went to the enemy camp and requested an interview with Holofernes. Judith told him that the Jews could not be conquered unless they had offended their God, but that they had indeed recently done just that and therefore God would abandon them. She promised to advise Holofernes when this would happen. Holofernes was very taken with Judith; he really fancied her and tried to persuade her to stay with him. She refused, but agreed that providing that she was allowed to leave the camp every day to bathe and pray, and was allowed to consume only the food and drink she had brought with her, she would otherwise remain within the camp to advise Holofernes as she had indicated.

On the 4th day she agreed to go to a feast given by Holofernes, though still taking only her own food. She:

> *"decked herself with her apparel and all her woman's attire and came and sat next to Holofernes. Holofernes' heart was ravished with her and his soul was moved and he desired exceedingly her company; and he was watching for a time to deceive her from the day he had seen her. And he said to her 'Drink now, and be merry with us.' And Judith said 'I will drink now my Lord,' but she ate and drank only what she had brought with her. And Holofernes took great delight in her and drank exceeding much wine, more than he had drunk at any one time in one day since he was born."*

Eventually alone with Judith, but drunk both with wine and her beauty, he passed out in a stupor on his own couch. Judith, calling on God for strength, then took his own sword and cut off his head; she put this in a bag for her maid to carry and the two of them went, apparently as usual, out of the camp and then to Bethulia. Received there with enthusiasm by the Jews, Judith instructed them to display the head over the town walls. They then mounted a raid on the enemy camp where, discovering that their general was dead, the army fled, leaving the camp to be looted. Judith dedicated her share of the plunder to God, remained a widow, and lived out the rest of her life in peace.

Serov simply re-tells this story in a 5-act work. Although it was commercially very successful for him, it is now rarely performed.

Susanna

In the Apocrypha of Daniel story, Susanna is the attractive wife of Joachim, a man highly regarded by his fellow Jews who were accustomed to meet in his house in the mornings to resolve lawsuits. Susanna's habit was to walk in the garden in the afternoons. Two Elders or Judges of the community observed her 'and were filled with love for her.' One hot afternoon when they had hidden in the garden Susanna, unaware of their presence instructed her maids to bring the necessary items so that she could bathe, and then dismissed them back to the house.

As soon as the maids had left, the two Elders revealed themselves:

"Behold the garden doors are shut that no man can see us, and we are in love with thee; therefore consent unto us and lie with us. If thou will not, we will bear witness against thee that a young man was with thee and therefore thou didst send thy maids away from thee."

Susanna refused, her maids ran out in response to her cries and the Elders, to protect themselves for they had not really expected this response, accused her as they had threatened. She was duly tried and sentenced to be stoned to death, this being the punishment for her alleged offence, for no one would refuse to believe the two Elders. However, in response to her prayers God sent an Angel who put 'a spirit of discernment upon a young man, this being Daniel'.

By taking separate testimony from the two Elders, Daniel showed them to be contradictory and deceitful:

> *"Then the whole synagogue shouted aloud in praise of the young man because from their own mouths he had proved them both to be confessedly false witnesses. And they dealt with them as the law prescribes, doing to them just as they maliciously intended against their sister."*

Which, by the laws of the times, meant that these Elders were themselves stoned to death. The Apocrypha story both demonstrates Daniel's wisdom and restores Susanna's reputation as a virtuous woman. Floyd's opera however focuses on Susannah (now spelt with an 'h') and the events of a few traumatic days in her life.

"Susannah"   Carlisle Floyd, 1955

Although the story is based on the tale in the Apocrypha of Daniel, it is transposed in time and place to a Tennessee valley in the 20th century.

In the first scene Susannah, a young, attractive, high-spirited girl, is having a great time at the local dance; she's very happy and full of fun. Unknowingly, however, she has attracted strong, sour criticism from the four Elders of the community and their wives. A stranger arrives and introduces himself as the Reverend Blitch, an itinerant preacher. The next day the four Elders, looking for a suitable creek which can be used by Blitch for baptisms, are stunned to see Susannah bathing in one, stark naked. After a few moments of staring at her like a group of peeping-toms, they recover their self-possession by telling themselves how shameless she is to be bathing naked in public, and that the people must be informed, to be protected against such wickedness.

That evening Susannah, quite unaware of what has happened, is frozen out by the community and, bewildered and hurt, she returns home. Little Bat arrives at Susannah's home. He is a simple, quiet 15-year-old youth generally ignored by the community but who adores Susannah. He explains to her what happened and why she has so suddenly been excluded. She is shocked, protesting that they must have been spying on her, for she frequently bathes there. However there is a lot worse to come for Little Bat confesses that, under heavy pressure from the Elders, their wives, and his own mother, he'd said that Susannah and he had had sexual contact, even though he knew it wasn't true. He'd been too scared to resist the pressure. That evening she goes to the church meeting to try to face people down. Reverend Blitch is there conducting a revivalist meeting and, seeing Susannah, he refers directly to her as a sinner in their midst and calls upon her to repent; she refuses and runs out into the night.

Later that evening she is alone on the porch of her home. Blitch approaches. They discuss her 'sin' and her refusal to atone for it. 'The Lord would've told me if I'd done something wrong'. Susannah, overwrought at everything that has happened to her in the last couple of days, suddenly breaks down, and collapses in tears. Blitch watches her, aware of an inner conflict in himself. He tells her that his is lonely work, that he's only human, that from time to time he has an overwhelming need of a woman. He asks if her brother will be at home. "No". Blitch lifts her, unresisting, to her feet. "Let's go inside," he says.

A few days later, Blitch is on his own in the church, kneeling and praying for forgiveness for having defiled an innocent, virginal young woman. The Elders and their wives enter. Blitch explains he has called them to this meeting to tell them they were wrong, he was wrong, about Susannah. But he cannot convince them without betraying himself, which of course he cannot do.

Sam returns home from hunting and Susannah tells him all that has happened, including her seduction/rape by Blitch. Sam is appalled at Blitch's hypocrisy, and taking a shot-gun he walks out to the creek where Blitch is conducting baptisms and shoots him. After this the community appear at Susannah's home and tell her she must leave the valley; however she refuses to be run out of her own home, and grabbing a gun sees them off her property. Only Little Bat remains. Slowly Susannah walks back, leans provocatively against a post, and invites him to come over to her for another spot of loving. Slowly, half-believingly, he puts an arm around her waist, only to receive a resounding slap, and runs off, to the sound of her laughter.

4. TALES FROM THE CROSS

Two of the most enduring legends concerning the crucifixion are those of the Wandering Jew (there is also a Wandering Jewess) and of the Holy Grail. The Wandering Jew seems to have made his first appearance in 1228 when, whilst in England, a visiting Bishop from Armenia reported on an encounter he had had with a man who called himself Cartaphilus and who claimed to have been a doorkeeper or porter to Pontius Pilate. According to the Bishop this man told him that he had struck Jesus whilst he was carrying the cross, telling him not to dawdle, and that Jesus had replied 'I am going, but you will wait upon my return'. Cartaphilus told the Bishop that thereafter he had lived and aged normally, but to the great age of 100; he had then metamorphosed to become a man of 30, which had been his age at the time of this event. He then aged normally again to 100, and again returned to be 30 years old and had continued this cycle ever since. Following this first appearance there have been a number of reported 'sightings' in various locations, the most recent being among the Mormons of Salt Lake City, Utah, in 1868.

Other versions of the same story tell of eye-witness accounts concerning a shoemaker named Ahasuerus who urged Jesus on at Golgotha and was told 'I shall stand and rest, but you shall know no rest'. The name Ahasuerus first seems to have been used in a pamphlet written in 1542, but the legend is the same of a Jew condemned to eternal wanderings on earth, or at least until Christ re-appears. A possible source of these tales lies within John's Gospel (18:22) which refers to Jesus being slapped by an interrogator.

Halévy, the Franco-Jewish composer of **La Juive,** used this story as the basis of **Le Juif Errant** ("The Wandering Jew"). A woman sings a ballad about a wandering Jew who can never die, who cannot stop anywhere for more than fifteen minutes, and who is continuously prodded on by the Avenging Angel with the words 'March, march.' The Jew (Ahasuerus), long repentant, hopes to earn his release and death by good deeds. To complete one of these he even fights with the Avenging Angel and as a result, feeling himself unusually weakened, happily awaits death. He hears singing and understands that it is a chorus of the dead and the damned, of devils and the blessed; at last, the Day of Judgement and his release has come. The Avenging Angel returns, revives Ahasuerus and orders him 'March, march'.

Wagner had already used the Wandering Jew legend in his opera *The Flying Dutchman,* a story with a very similar theme of a man condemned to wander the Earth (in this case sail the seas) forever; and of his longing for death, and hope of redemption. The Dutchman is doomed to sail the world alone in his ship for eternity because he had had the temerity to swear an oath "by all the devils" and the Devil, taking offence, reversed the curse in this way. The Dutchman has but one forlorn hope for release from his sentence; he is allowed to put into port for a day once every seven years and if, during this brief stay, he can find a young woman who will, for love of him, sacrifice herself to be with him, they will both die together. In his various writings Wagner acknowledged the association of this story to the Wandering Jew legend.

He also, in *Lohengrin,* briefly touched on the other of these two well-known legends, that of the Holy Grail, when at the end of the opera Lohengrin reveals his name and that he is the son of Parsifal, King of the Grail Knights. The Holy Grail is, in these legends, the cup or chalice from which Christ drank at his Last Supper, and which in some versions was also used to catch his blood whilst he was on the cross.

Operatically, Lohengrin pre-dates his father Parsifal by over 30 years and during this time Wagner's anti-semitism went from sheer prejudice to virulent hatred, reaching the point where, in *Parsifal*, he even appears to attempt to separate Christianity from its Jewish origins and to 'purify' Christ from his Jewish blood. He seemed to try to use the opera to develop his beliefs that the pure Aryan German was descended from the gods, whereas the rest of the world came from Darwin's apes. (No wonder Hitler was a great admirer of his!) 'Christianity arranged for Wagner' was Nietzsche's sardonic comment. An ironic twist arose in the preparations for the first performance; Wagner was too short of funds to be able to mount *Parsifal* himself, but his long-time patron King Ludwig II of Bavaria provided a substantial sum of money, together with the free use of the Munich Opera's orchestra and chorus, and also the services of its conductor to produce the new work. Gratefully accepting, Wagner did not realise at the time that the conductor was one Hermann Levi, son of a rabbi! His struggles to rid himself of Levi, fruitless though they were, for Ludwig would have no truck with Wagner's anti-semitism, caused him to write what were, even by his standards, some of his most rabid letters on the subject.

"Parsifal"   Wagner, 1882

In this, his final opera, Wagner combined the Grail story with yet another of these crucifixion legends, this concerning a Roman soldier who supposedly wounded Christ on the cross with his spear, and of the supernatural powers which the spear thus acquired. The Holy Grail and the Sacred Spear are central to the working of the Parsifal story.

Titurel is the leader of a group of Knights who are the keepers of the Holy Grail and the Sacred Spear; the Knights guard these Relics in their mountain castle. Nearby lives Klingsor, a pagan magician who wants possession of both the Grail and the Spear. He has created a magic garden inhabited by beautiful young girls; the Knights, committed to total spiritual and sexual purity, are often lured to the destruction of this ideal by these girls. Klingsor also has total power over a beautiful woman, Kundry, who was condemned to live forever after laughing at Christ whilst he was carrying the cross. When not being forced to serve Klingsor, Kundry tries to work at Titurel's castle, unrecognised, as a lowly penitent servant, hoping somehow for salvation or redemption.

Before the opera really begins, we learn that Titurel is old and has handed over his responsibilities to his son Amfortas. Wanting to destroy Klingsor, Amfortas has taken the Spear and gone to Klingsor's domain where he was waylaid and seduced by Kundry. Klingsor picked up the Spear which Amfortas had dropped and wounded him with it. Amfortas was rescued by Gurnemanz and other Knights, but his wound will not heal. Weakened and debilitated by the wound and its associated pain, Amfortas is unable to carry out his regular duty of unveiling the Grail.

These events arc told many years later by Gurnemanz, now himself getting old, to some young Knights. He adds that Amfortas, in his prayers for forgiveness of his sin, has received a prophecy of redemption through a 'guileless fool' who would someday arrive at the castle.

A young man arrives who doesn't even know his own name. Gurnemanz senses the realisation of the prophecy and takes him to witness the ceremony of the unveiling of the Grail. However, it means nothing to the young man and in disgust Gurnemanz throws him out of the castle. He travels to Klingsor's domain, where he is completely unaffected by the distractions offered by the girls in the magic garden; Klingsor sends Kundry to seduce him. She calls him 'Parsifal', and he immediately knows that this is his name. Failing to seduce him, she calls for help from Klingsor, who hurls the Spear at him. Parsifal catches it, makes the sign of the cross with it, and Klingsor and his domain disintegrate.

Years later Parsifal reappears at Titurel's castle bearing the Spear. Gurnemanz is now very old but recognises him and realises that fulfilment of the prophecy is at hand. Kundry too recognises Parsifal; she washes his feet, dries them with her hair, and is given absolution by him. Seeing Amfortas still unhealed, Parsifal touches the wound with the Spear and it immediately heals. Gurnemanz anoints Parsifal as the new King of the Grail Knights, the Grail itself is unveiled, and Kundry dies. Redemption indeed.

A major allegorical work such as this accrues many interpretations and **Parsifal** has received its full share. Kundry of course is in one respect an incarnation of the Wandering Jewess, yet another of these Christological legends, about the woman who supposedly laughed at Christ on his way to execution. Her final actions of washing and drying Parsifal's feet echo the Gospels of John (12:3-7) and Luke (7:37-38) concerning the actions of Mary of Bethany, and Mary the repentant prostitute; the Pope decided in 1854 that these were both the same woman, also known as Mary Magdalene, and this association raises Kundry to an even more significant status in Wagner's allegory.

For all its importance in the Wagner canon, and supposed religious significance, it has also been said of this work that: "*Parsifal* is the kind of opera that starts at 6 o'clock. After it has been going for three hours you look at your watch and it says 6:20."

(David Randolph: *American Treasury* 1955).

5. ALL RIGHT-THINKING PEOPLE ...

With religion, intolerance can mean real hatred, differences can mean disaster, and acts of transgression can mean death. One might think that Jews and Christians for instance, who share the same God and belief in a Messiah, might have been able to reach an accommodation over their differing views about the Messiah, instead of entering into 2000 years of still unfinished persecutions and hatreds. As a result they had, by the early Middle Ages, reached a stage of social intercourse such that, if a Jew married "out", i.e. to a Christian, the family would regard their child as having died, would go through a period of ritual mourning, and never again have contact with their "dead" offspring, such was the gravity of the offence. Christians viewed marriage to a Jew in much the same way, except that in some parts of their world they did not fool about with assumed death; these Christians simply put to death all the parties to such a marriage --- the bride, the groom, and the officials; there was scarcely a greater sin than to marry a Jew. In 1350 the Bishop of Orvieto, in Central Italy, softened this position by decreeing more mercifully that if a Jew and a Christian came together in a love affair, then instead of executing all those involved, only the woman (whichever her faith) was to be put to death, by beheading or by being burnt alive! Pope Callixtus III (the first Borgia Pope) revived legislation that had been allowed to lapse; he banned all social intercourse between Christians and Jews. Even today some of these attitudes still linger, particularly among some groups of orthodox Jews, and have been nicely illustrated in the modern musical *Fiddler on the Roof.*

This total mutual hostility between Christian and Jew is at the heart of one of the grandest of grand operas, **La Juive** (*The Jewess*) by Halévy.

Religious hatreds however are not limited to relationships between these two faiths; absolute intolerance between Catholic and Protestant Christians is still very much alive and kicking, as the Northern Ireland situation demonstrates. These two groups, who both accept "love thy neighbour" as a religious precept, continue to murder and maim each other over the differences in their beliefs just as easily today as they did in the 16th century at the time of the Huguenot massacre in Paris, an event which is the focus of Meyerbeer's *Les Huguenots*. Christians went to war against Islam in the Crusades because of the "heretical" nature of that faith and to "liberate" Jerusalem from the Muslims and Jews; Verdi wrote *I Lombardi* around that subject. In India the (Christian) British tried to suppress Hinduism and for their pains have found this attempt recorded in operatic history in Delibes' *Lakmé*. Conflict between Hindu and Muslim is the background to *The King of Lahore* by Massenet; and so the list goes on.

"La Juive" *("The Jewess")* **Halévy, 1835**

The action is in Constance in 1414 at the time of the Easter and Passover festivals. The people are celebrating the return of Prince Léopold from his latest victory.

Act 1 Some Christians angrily confront Eléazar, a Jewish goldsmith, and his daughter Rachel for working on a public holiday, accusing them of blasphemy. Eléazar responds equally angrily by pointing out that he is a Jew, not bound to Christian observances, and that anyway since the Christians had arranged that his sons were burned at the stake in front of him, he has no love for Christianity. Cardinal Brogni, the prelate of the city, arrives and he and Eléazar recognise each other from their past in Rome. Brogni was then a magistrate, not a minister of religion, with a wife and baby daughter, but had lost his family and possessions in a fire tragedy. He is reminded that he had expelled Eléazar from Rome. Now, in a conciliatory gesture Brogni pardons Eléazar for his current offence and offers friendship, which Eléazar silently scorns. Later Eléazar and Rachel are again rescued from the angry crowd, but now by Rachel's friend Samuel, a Jewish painter who visits her and whom she has come to love. He seems to have an extraordinary influence over the crowd.

Act 2 In Eléazar's house they are celebrating the Passover with Samuel, and Rachel notices how uncomfortable he seems with the Passover food and rituals. There is a knock on the door; the table is rapidly cleared and Samuel hastily conceals himself. Princess Eudoxie enters to order some extravagant jewellery for her returning husband Prince Léopold, to be delivered the next day. When the princess leaves, Rachel challenges Samuel over his behaviour; he confesses that he loves her but admits too that he is not Jewish, hence his unfamiliarity with the Passover rituals. In spite of this, and the knowledge of the fate awaiting those who enter into a Jewish/Christian marriage, Rachel loves him too much to give him up and prevails on her father to accept him too, and allow them to marry. To their shock and horror Samuel refuses marriage.

Act 3 Eléazar and Rachel go to deliver the jewellery ordered by Princess Eudoxie for Léopold and are appalled to discover that Léopold is none other than Samuel! Outraged at the deception, Rachel denounces him for having seduced a Jewess --- herself. Cardinal Brogni becomes involved, and because of the gravity of the offence pronounces Anathema, the ultimate curse, upon Eléazar, Rachel and Léopold. He then calls upon God to curse all Jews, and sentences the three of them to death.

Act 4 In prison awaiting execution, Rachel is visited by Princess Eudoxie, who pleads with her to save Léopold's life by recanting the accusation of seduction. Reflecting that both of them love Léopold but that only she, the despised Jewess, can save him, Rachel agrees to do this for the sake of the love she still bears him.

Brogni tries to do his Christian duty by telling Eléazar that his life and that of his daughter will be spared if they will become Christians. Eléazar treats this offer with contempt; he is ready to die, only before dying he wants revenge on Brogni. He then proceeds to gain this by telling Brogni that he, Eléazar, was present all those years ago in Rome when Brogni's house burned, and that he saw a Jew rescue the baby girl, that he knows this Jew, and "No", he's not going to tell Brogni who it is. Later, having thought long and hard on whether or not to tell Rachel about Brogni's offer to save her life, and soliloquising in the best-known aria in the whole opera "Rachelle, quand du Seigneur...", Eléazar finally decides he must give her the opportunity.

Act 5 He does this as they are being led out to their execution. Rachel scorns the offer as vehemently as did her father: "Come, the flames sparkle" is her response. Brogni quietly speaks to Eléazar, begging, urgently pleading, for information about his daughter. At least he asks "Tell me if she is still alive." Eléazar, his eyes on Rachel, says "Yes, she is". As Rachel is thrown into the flames, Brogni pleads again: "Where is she?" "There!" says Eléazar, pointing to her.

"Les Huguenots"   Meyerbeer, 1836

Act 1 The setting is Paris in 1572, the year of the massacre of the Huguenots (a Protestant sect) by the Catholics in that city. In the background to events the Catholic Princess Marguerite de Valois, the King's sister, is engaged to the Huguenot Prince Henri de Navarre and sees her marriage as an example of how to reduce the simmering religious tensions between the Catholics and Protestants. She decides to arrange a marriage between Raoul, a loyal Huguenot nobleman, and Valentine, daughter of the equally loyal Catholic Count de Saint-Bris. But there is an initial problem to be overcome; Valentine is already engaged to the Count of Nevers, also a Catholic.

The Count is at his home with a group of fellow-Catholic friends; they are expecting Raoul. Although he is a Huguenot, they resolve to welcome him as a friend. When he arrives, he tells them that on his way there he was instrumental in rescuing a beautiful young woman from the attentions of a group of rowdies and, in a lyrical aria, he describes her charms and attractions, finally lamenting that he has absolutely no idea who she is.

A mysterious young woman arrives and insists on a private meeting with Nevers in the gardens. The young men, looking out of the window, all agree that Nevers has a new mistress, but only Raoul recognises her: she is the girl he rescued earlier. In his distress over her presumed relationship with Nevers, he does not hear Nevers return and explain to his friends that the girl is Valentine de Saint-Bris, his fiancée, who came to tell him that, obeying the wishes of Marguerite, she must break off their engagement, and that he had no option but to agree.

Act 2 In Marguerite's apartments, Valentine arrives and tells her that the engagement is over. Raoul arrives in response to a summons, and is told of the plan: Marguerite wishes him to marry an heiress, the daughter of his life-long enemy the Catholic Count de Saint-Bris, as a practical step towards renouncing their mutual hatreds and introducing a measure of religious peace. Raoul accepts, as do Nevers and Saint-Bris, the merits of this plan and agrees to the marriage. Valentine is then brought in. To Raoul's horror he sees that the girl he is being invited to marry in the name of religious peace is none other than Nevers' presumed mistress, and he flatly refuses her. There is total shock all round; Raoul is appalled at what he sees as the gross insult to himself, whilst the Catholics are outraged at the offence he has given, the insult to Valentine, to her father Saint-Bris, and to her ex-fiancé, Nevers. They all unite in calling for blood --- and in particular Raoul's blood --- to avenge the situation.

Act 3 With the collapse of Marguerite's plan, Nevers and Valentine re-establish their engagement and agree to marry immediately. Saint-Bris swears to have revenge on Raoul, and he and his friends immediately put into place a scheme to entrap Raoul that day and ensure his death. Nevers is excluded from this plan because of his wedding to Valentine that afternoon. However, Valentine has overheard the plotting and sends Raoul a warning. A duel between Saint-Bris and Raoul is interrupted by the arrival of Marguerite who commands the peace. Accusations and explanations are made and demanded, particularly from Raoul on why he would not marry Valentine. He explains his reason and is rapidly disabused by Marguerite, who tells him what the situation really was.

Act 4 At the home of Count Nevers, Valentine, now Countess Nevers, is distressed and in a long and delicate aria she blames her father for insisting on the marriage, for she realises now that she loves Raoul.

Raoul appears, having secretly entered the house determined, as he tells her, to see her before he dies. Hearing her father and husband approaching, Valentine insists that he hides. Saint-Bris, Nevers and others assemble to review their plan to massacre the Huguenots whom, they tell each other, God has sentenced to death. Saint-Bris tells Nevers that he is to lead the killing. This Nevers refuses to do and is arrested on Saint-Bris' orders, to be held until after the massacre. The monks among the group provide religious support for Saint-Bris' tactics, crying anathema upon the Huguenots and calling for the slaughter also to include the women and children. When they leave, Raoul is about to go too, to warn the Huguenots, but Valentine detains him. He will only be killed, she says; he just wants to fight her father and her husband, and besides, she tells him, 'I love you'. Raoul is astounded and delighted, but still must leave to warn his co-religionists. He finally extricates himself from her arms and dashes off.

Act 5 The Huguenots are celebrating Marguerite's marriage when Raoul rushes in with news of the imminent attack. Valentine appears, saying that she can save Raoul, but he must become a Catholic! "Never! And anyway where is your husband?" "Dead --- murdered!" Raoul is now torn between his duty to fight with his friends, or to save himself and flee with the woman he loves, who is now so suddenly and unexpectedly free to marry him. In a final desperate plea, Valentine says that since he won't adopt her faith she'll adopt his, even though it may cost her her soul, so that they can at least be together in life. With this promise Raoul is persuaded and they escape, but hear the sound of advancing soldiers. As they are discovered, Raoul is killed and Valentine mortally wounded, though she lives long enough for the officer in charge of the soldiers, none other than Saint-Bris, to realise that he has just killed his own daughter.

"Stiffelio"   Verdi, 1850

The opera concerns a group of Ahasuerans, a minor Protestant sect that has historically itself suffered intolerant persecution by mainstream Christianity. The setting and nature of some of the action, and the dramatic background of a church, attracted the active hostility of the religious censors of the day, forcing major revisions on Verdi. The closing moments of the opera are of a movingly Christian act of forgiveness and tolerance.

Thou shalt not commit adultery. This, the seventh of God's Ten Commandments to Moses in Sinai, is at the heart of the drama and passions of this opera. For while Stiffelio, the Minister of the Ahasueran community, is away on a preaching mission, this is just what his wife Lina does in his absence; she has an adulterous relationship with a member of the community, to the deep shame of her father, and to the shock and fury of Stiffelio when this is discovered on his return. The opera concerns the working-out of this situation within an intensely religious sect who try to keep all their everyday thoughts and actions in a totally biblical context.

The opera opens with one of the Ministers reading his Bible and reflecting on its inspired prophecies. It ends with Stiffelio at his pulpit, with his entire congregation present, including Lina, reading directly from the Bible the Gospel about Christ's words concerning the woman taken in adultery.

Lina wants to confess and explain to Stiffelio, but first her father's pride prevents her, then Stiffelio's coldness and hostility make it impossible. He compels her to sign a document that supposedly is a contract of divorce, and Lina takes the opportunity to force him to hear her confession, which he has been reluctant to do. For now that she is no longer his wife, she can turn to Stiffelio in his capacity as her Minister and require that he perform his religious duty and hear her confession. And this was an action which was regarded by the religious authorities as simply sacrilegious; the words 'Minister, Minister' were unacceptable in this context to them. They could not allow such a solemn process as a religious confession to be enacted on a public stage. It would cause a scandal.

Stiffelio is confused by events and by Lina's confession to him. In the church that evening he walks past her and does not even recognise her. He mounts the pulpit, his Bible falls open at random, and he starts reading:-

'Then Jesus, turning to the assembled people, pointed to the adulteress at
his feet and said ...
Whichever of you is without sin
Let him cast the first stone ...
And the woman... the woman rose up forgiven ...
Forgiven ... forgiven ... forgiven
God has spoken it.'

Stiffelio is looking at his wife as he reads, his expression and gestures as much as the words showing that he has accepted Christ's teaching here.

This too, this staged presentation of a classic Christian action of forgiveness following the teaching of Jesus Christ himself, could not be tolerated by the religious authorities because again of the supposed sanctity of the words of Christ and his message. It was a profanity to present this on a public stage, and even worse to use the setting of a church.

As a result of the changes forced upon Verdi, the opera was not successful and was effectively lost until relatively recently, when it was "rediscovered" and is enjoying increasing recognition and popularity.

The Crusades

Verdi's next work after his hugely successful **Nabucco** was the clumsily titled **I Lombardi alla Prima Crociata** ("The Lombards at the First Crusade"); it is generally known now by the more practical abbreviated version **I Lombardi.** The action and storyline centre (after Act 1) on a force of militant Christians from the Lombardy Plain who have joined the first army of Crusaders to Palestine in 1096/7, intent on driving the heretic Jews and Muslims out of Jerusalem and perhaps also destroying the Muslim religion.

We have seen Christian/Jewish hatreds at work in *La Juive,* and Catholic/Protestant prejudice in *Les Huguenots;* **I Lombardi** is an instance of specifically Christian/Muslim antipathies. It is interesting that the Christian religion, so profoundly based on precepts of peace, love and tolerance, can also be the basis of so much savagery, hatred and intolerance, not only towards other religions but also between differing Christian creeds, so much so that these negative influences are widely commented on even in such a narrow art-form as opera. But perhaps it illustrates also how wide is the distance between the Son of God and those he came to save, and how great is their need of him. Historically, one of the tragedies of the Crusades is that, a full 1000 years after Christ's lifetime, his message had become so distorted that men would travel hundreds of miles to kill those who preferred a different message.

The Crusades --- the word comes from *"croisiere"*, a cross of red material sewn onto the shoulders of the men's jerkins to signify they were Soldiers of Christ --- were initiated by Pope Urban II at the Council of Clermont in 1095. The Council comprised, it was said, 14 Archbishops, 250 Bishops, and 400 Abbots; large numbers of knights and their men were in attendance. The Pope exhorted the Council to rid the Holy City of Jerusalem of its Muslims and Jews, and the assembled clerics responded enthusiastically with affirmations that 'God wills it'.

The First Crusade of Verdi's opera however nearly didn't make it; a huge rag-tag of an advance party was savagely reduced as it pillaged and massacred its way across Europe, and was finally crushed by the Turks after the remnant crossed the Bosphorus. Four following armies however, supported by what proved to be very necessary naval back-up, made up for this by fighting their way finally to Jerusalem, where they slaughtered some 70,000 Muslims and Jews of all ages and both sexes.

"I Lombardi"   Verdi, 1843

Act 1 *"The Revenge"* Arvino and Pagano are brothers but Pagano had tried to murder Arvino and was exiled; there is now a service of reconciliation going on in the Cathedral in Milan. Pagano however privately still intends to kill Arvino. Meanwhile, a priest arrives with news of a Crusade to rid Jerusalem of its Muslim occupants and that Arvino has been appointed to lead the Lombard army.

Scene 2. In their father's palace Pagano again tries to murder Arvino but again fails; this time he mistakenly kills their father instead. Now, absolutely appalled at what he has done, he flees from the city, genuinely horror-struck at the enormity of his crime.

Act 2 *"The Man of the Cave"*. It is Antioch, *Syria* ("and it was first in Antioch that the Disciples were by divine providence called Christians" --- Acts 11:26) in the palace of Acciano, Tyrant of Antioch. The people are discussing the arrival of the Crusaders and assuring themselves that Allah's thunderbolts will punish the infidels. Sofia, Acciano's wife, has been secretly baptised; Oronte, their son, has fallen for the beautiful

Christian girl Giselda, captured from the invading Crusaders and now held in Acciano's harem. They enter discussing Giselda and Sofia's hopes that Oronte will become a convert.

Scene 2 - A Christian hermit emerges from a nearby cave. A man approaches who identifies himself as Pirra, a Lombard who assisted at a crime of parricide and fled to Syria, renouncing his faith. He has sought out the famed saintly hermit for help. He mentions that he has charge of the walls of Antioch. Hearing the sounds of the approaching Crusaders, the hermit tells Pirra that to atone for his sin he must open its walls to the Crusaders. Pirra agrees, promising to do it himself.

A group of Lombards arrives, forcing Pirra to take refuge in the hermit's cave. They are led by Arvino, who is searching for his lost daughter Giselda, captured by a band of Muslims. The hermit promises Arvino that he will indeed see his daughter again and the scene ends with a couple of choruses ridiculing Allah and glorifying God.

Scene 3 - In the harem of Acciano's palace, Giselda is suddenly informed by Sofia that both her husband Acciano and her son Oronte have been killed by the invading Christians, who were able to penetrate the city through treachery. Arvino and his men enter. Giselda, shocked by hearing of the death of Oronte, whom she has fallen for, is now appalled by the bloody appearance of her father and his soldiers, who were clearly involved in the killing of Oronte; she reacts furiously against her father's killings. Completely taken aback by her anger, and with his bloodlust at a high, he is only prevented from killing her too by being persuaded that his daughter is out of her mind.

Act 3 *"The Conversion."* The opening scene is set in the valley of Jehoshaphat, with views of the hills of Jerusalem and the Mount of Olives. Giselda appears, unable to stand the atmosphere in her father's tent; then Oronte stumbles on stage. Clearly not dead after all, as his mother had thought and Giselda had believed, he had been badly wounded and had since been wandering about in the hope of finding Giselda. They promise themselves to each other and Oronte also promises to worship her God. They hear the sounds of Crusaders nearby and run.

Scene 2 - In his tent Arvino swears vengeance against Pagano, who has been seen in the vicinity, and calls on God to deal with his daughter.

Scene 3 - A grotto near the banks of the Jordan. The action is introduced by a long and beautiful violin solo and concludes with an equally melodic trio. Giselda is supporting Oronte, who is dying from his wounds. The hermit appears, promising Oronte a new life if he will convert to Christianity. Having already promised Giselda that he would do just that, Oronte readily agrees and is baptised from the waters of Jordan. However his new life is to be elsewhere, for he promptly dies of his wounds. (This scene almost caused trouble at its première because the Archbishop of Milan, hearing of the baptismal sequence, tried to have it banned as being sacrilegious.)

Act 4 "*The Holy Sepulchre*". Giselda in a dream has a vision of Oronte who tells her that he is on his way to Heaven, and that her people, who are very short of water, should go to the fountain of Siloam where they will find fresh water. She awakes, and in the cabaletta *Non fu sogno!* that is possibly the best-known number in the whole opera sings in celebration that it was not a dream

Scene 2 - The Lombard tents near Rachel's tomb. In a chorus "O Signore, dal tetto natio" which echoes the sentiments of the "Va pensiero" chorus in *Nabucco*, the parched, thirsty Crusaders and pilgrims recall the pleasures and benefits of the Lombard fields against their present place where "the sand of an arid soil is harsher and more burning to our lips". It also has quite attractive music and deserves to be better known. Giselda, Arvino and the hermit appear, calling "To Siloam! To Siloam!" Water is gushing from Siloam.

Scene 3 - Arvino's tent. He and Giselda enter, supporting the mortally wounded hermit, who had fought in the forefront of battle. He is dazed and confused, but tells Arvino that hc is his brother Pagano, now close to death and seeking forgiveness. They are reconciled, and Pagano dies.

6. DON CARLOS and the AUTO da FÉ

It took Christianity a little over 1000 years to feel strong enough and confident enough to start throwing its weight around as a proselytising faith. Peaceful conversion by persuasion virtually came to an end for a while with the Crusades, which were a deliberate attempt by Pope Urban II and his successors, using force, both to liberate Jerusalem from the heretics and to kill as many of them as possible. For several centuries afterwards religious conversion by force of arms, control of the "faithful" by terror, and complete corruption through total power became the hallmarks of Church expansion. One of its most fearsome weapons of control was the Inquisition, an institution which established a reign of terror, most notably in Spain, lasting hundreds of years. It operated on a scale of savagery and corruption, extending over the whole of the Christian world, that had never been seen before and has not been seen since; indeed the only available, and most commonly used comparison today to indicate its level of horror is to place the Inquisition alongside the Holocaust. It was set up by Pope Gregory IX specifically to fight heresy, witchcraft and other deviations from the "truth", and its position was subsequently strengthened by Pope Innocent IV when he authorised the use of torture to obtain confessions.

A principal tool of the Inquisition was the *Auto da Fé* (from the Portuguese term meaning Act of Faith). In the procedure that became the Auto da Fé heretics were called upon to recant their heresy, thus performing the "Acts of Faith". The public were encouraged to witness this act by developing the ceremony into an occasion of considerable pomp, grandeur and ultimately horror, for its climax became to carry out death sentences by a ritual burning at the stake. Eventually the

Auto da Fé came to mean this form of public execution. The first of these "acts of faith" was in Seville in 1481, and the last was in Mexico in 1850, so the practice went on for almost 400 years.

The ceremony was designed as a spectacular, usually taking place in the main square of the town, in the presence of royalty wherever possible, otherwise the Governor or whoever represented the ultimate civil authority for the area. There would be a lengthy procession, a solemn mass, an oath of obedience to the Inquisition, a sermon, and the reading of the sentences. Those who had been condemned to death wore the *san benito,* the yellow garment embroidered both with a cross and the symbols of their particular heresies. Commonly these victims were lapsed converts, former Jews and Muslims who had been found to have been insincere in their conversions. The Inquisition actually had no power to impose the death penalty, for there was a fiction that the Church could not let blood. The victims were therefore handed over to the civil authorities for sentencing, with a suitable plea from the Inquisition that these authorities should be merciful (this after the confession of heresy had been obtained by the Inquisitor's torturers, presumably without a letting of blood). Mercy could be shown of course, for if a victim's family were wealthy enough they would bribe an official to garotte the sinner before the fires became too fierce.

It has been estimated that during the almost 400-year period of the Inquisition some 40-50,000 people were put to death in this way in Spain alone, and of these perhaps 2000 died at the instigation of the first Inquisitor General of Spain, one Tomás de Torquemada, whose name still rings down the centuries with the sound of the terror his atrocities generated. Over the rest of Europe it has been estimated that more than 150,000 people died at the hands of (or at the instigation of) the Inquisition in just one 10-year period alone. This, together with Catholic repression of Protestants in Flanders, is the religious background to **Don Carlos**.

The Don Carlos of the opera however, whilst still the son and heir of King Philip, is not given the character of the historical Don; this was a boy whose mother had died whilst he was still a child and who was then brought up by two aunts, hardly seeing his father until he was about 14. He was an epileptic who had very poor health and an even poorer disposition, being almost pathologically vicious and unstable. His character traits were such that before long Philip declared him unsuitable as a future king and debarred him from the succession. Carlos attempted to gain revenge by joining a plot against his father but was arrested and imprisoned. A few months later he died in the prison, at the early age of 23. His more normal --- though weak-willed --- operatic counterpart also rebels against his father and is imprisoned, but neither his interest in the plight of the Protestants nor his blighted romance with his stepmother Elisabeth have any basis in history.

The ceremonial of the Auto da Fé and the later appearance of the Grand Inquisitor are just two of the scenes that make Verdi's **Don Carlos** the epitome of grand opera. It is set in 16th-century Spain in the reign of King Philip II, the man who for four years was also King Philip of England by virtue of his marriage to Queen ("Bloody") Mary of England, Henry VIII's elder daughter and half-sister to her successor Queen Elizabeth I. The opera sets scenes of frustrated love and political intrigue against a background of religious persecution of the Protestant Hollanders; there is also the struggle for supremacy between the King's temporal power and the claims of the Church --- represented by the Inquisition --- to everlasting and over-riding spiritual power.

Don Carlos has it all: a story of a lost love and a forlorn lover, a jealous woman, a loveless marriage, a suspicious and neurotic King, spectacular pageantry, murder, adultery and some of the most dramatic and lyrical music Verdi ever wrote. And complementing this complex story and wonderful music is a libretto of equal stature, based on a play by the German poet Schiller. It is my personal favourite of all the operas I have ever seen or listened to. The piece was originally written as a long 5-act work to a libretto in French, but Verdi later reduced it to 4-acts with an Italian libretto written for him by Antonio Ghislanzoni, with whom he had worked before and was to work again (on *Aida*). Ghislanzoni himself was also an unusually talented man; not only a skilled writer who could provide Verdi with exactly what he wanted, but also a writer on his own account, a doctor, a musician (he played the double-bass), and the possessor of a baritone voice good enough for him to sing in opera.

"Don Carlos"   Verdi, 1867

Act 1 The Forest of Fontainebleau. Carlos is the heir to the throne of his father, the powerful though widowed King Philip of Spain; he is due to be married to Elisabeth of France in what would have been an arranged political marriage, though when they meet they fall in love. However a courier arrives with the news that, to strengthen the newly achieved peace between France and Spain, it has been decided that Elisabeth should instead marry King Philip in order to cement an even stronger alliance. In the interests of the peace Elisabeth agrees. (This Act 1 meeting between Carlos and Elisabeth is in the original, 1867 5-act version, but the entire sequence was excised by Verdi in 1884 when he reduced the work to 4 acts).

Act 2 Scene 1. The Cloisters of the San Yuste Monastery. Carlos notices the remarkable resemblance of one of the monks to his late grandfather Emperor Charles V, who was not only King of Spain but was also the Holy Roman Emperor. He tells his friend Rodrigo, Marquis de Posa, of his love for Elisabeth but is told by Rodrigo, lately returned from Flanders and deeply disturbed by what he has seen there, to try and think of other things, like taking up the cause of the oppressed Flemish people who are suffering severely under King Philip's determined and bloody enforcement of Catholicism.

Scene 2. Near the gates of the Monastery. The Princess Eboli and other members of the Court pass the time with "The Veil Song"; they are joined by Elisabeth, and then Posa, who requests an audience with Elisabeth for Carlos; this prompts Eboli to think that Carlos might be in love with her. Carlos appears, Elisabeth dismisses everyone, hears him out and agrees to help persuade the King to let him go to Flanders. Carlos however then simply allows his frustrated love for his step-mother to get the better of him and behaves like a callow youth in his pleas to her, before going off. The King enters. Philip, a lonely and suspicious man, isolated by his power, is angry at finding the Queen alone, without her lady-in-waiting: he demands to know who the missing lady is and immediately dismisses her, ordering her back to France, indifferent to his wife's protests. Suspicious even of his son's relationship with Elisabeth, he requests Rodrigo to keep an eye on them. Rodrigo takes the opportunity to urge Philip to relax his oppressive regime in Flanders. 'Why?' asks the King, at least things are quiet there now. 'It's the silence of the grave' replies Rodrigo in an emotional response. Impressed by his sincerity, yet showing unusual concern for him and his opinions, Philip advises him to watch out for the Grand Inquisitor.

Act 3 *Scene 1. The Queen's Gardens.* Carlos goes to a secret meeting with (as he thinks) Elisabeth after having received an anonymous note; the woman he meets is masked but wearing the Queen's clothes, and Carlos declares his love for her. But the woman is Princess Eboli; there are festivities, for the next day is Philip's coronation and the Queen, preferring to rest, asked Eboli to stand in for her, providing her with a mask and suitable clothes. Eboli exploited the opportunity to arrange a secret meeting with Carlos by sending him the note, believing him to be in love with her. But realising from his words the real direction of his emotions, she determines on revenge for the humiliation which she has brought on herself.

Scene 2. A large Square by the Cathedral. There is an Auto da Fé (a Verdi spectacular) at which the Flemish officials, with Carlos, ask Philip to show mercy; Posa, the Queen, and much of the crowd support this plea. Philip flatly refuses, so Carlos then asks directly to be sent to Flanders. Again Philip refuses. Angered now, Carlos draws his sword and appears to threaten the man who is not only his father, but is also the all-powerful and autocratic King. Rodrigo intervenes, persuades Carlos to hand over his sword, and is instantly created a Duke for this service. Meanwhile the Auto da Fé continues.

Act 4 *Scene 1. The King's Study.* In one of the most impressive scenes in all opera, Philip is alone in his study reflecting on his unhappiness and the fact that even his wife doesn't love him, when the Grand Inquisitor is announced. The duet between these two is unique in being a scene written for two basses, who for a while are the only people on the stage; it is intensely dramatic and powerfully written, both in the music and the libretto. The Inquisitor demands that Philip hand over to him his son Carlos, so that the heresies implicit in Carlos' words and actions at the Auto da Fé can be investigated. Even though his son's religious sympathies are clearly suspect by reason of his support for the Flemish, and even though he has committed the outrageous offence of threatening the King, Philip hesitates. The Inquisitor's demand means certain death for Carlos. 'Must I then even give up my son?' he asks, to which the Inquisitor responds forcefully that God himself did just that. Philip has no answer to this and agrees not only that Carlos will be put to death but also that Rodrigo, Carlos' friend, will be handed over as a heretic because he too is clearly a supporter of the Flemish.

As the Inquisitor leaves, Elisabeth rushes in saying that her jewel box has been stolen and demands the King's help in recovering it. Philip himself produces it and insists that she open it, in front of him. It contains a portrait of Don Carlos, and Philip uses this as evidence of her adultery with Carlos. Elisabeth emphatically denies this, pointing out that she retained the portrait because she was once going to be married to him. Eboli enters, confessing that it was she who stole the jewel box intent on causing trouble for both Carlos and the Queen; she further confesses that she has been having an adulterous affair with the King. Elisabeth orders her from the Court and into exile or a convent; in the famous aria "O don fatale", Eboli chooses the convent, in penitence.

Scene 2. A Prison. Rodrigo visits Carlos in prison and tells him that he, Rodrigo, has implicated himself as one of the leaders of the Flemish revolt so that with luck Carlos will be freed. Two men are seen entering the prison, a shot is fired and Rodrigo falls, mortally wounded. Before he dies he is able to tell Don Carlos that Elisabeth will meet him the next day in the convent of San Yuste. The King enters, to return Carlos' sword to him, but Carlos wants nothing to do with his father.

Act 5 The Monastery of San Yuste. Elisabeth and Carlos, recognising inevitability, make their last farewells to each other. Philip and the Grand Inquisitor quietly enter with guards and take hold of both of them. The Inquisitor pronounces Anathema upon Carlos but he manages to escape the guards and retreats towards the tomb of Charles V, which suddenly opens and the monk from Act 2 appears. He is recognised as the ghost of Charles V, Carlos' grandfather, who leads Carlos to safety.

7. TO THE DEVIL WITH OPERA

"Madam, I know you are a veritable devil, but I would have you know that I am Beelzebub, the Head Devil."
Handel, to the singer Francesca Cuzzoni
during rehearsals.

The word "devil" derives from the Greek "diabolos" meaning slanderer or accuser, though it is now often used to mean any one of the many creatures serving Beelzebub - the Head Devil, otherwise known simply as "The Devil". "Beelzebub" is only one of the Devil's many names; originally he was known as *Satan* (from the Hebrew "Shatan", or adversary). In early Biblical times Satan was not the Devil as we think of him today, but a member of God's 'court' with the role of prosecutor, or adversary (hence "devil's advocate", although today's use of the term is more literally applied to the official appointed by the Papal Consistory to find reasons why a person should not be made a saint). He appears in this role in the *Book of Job*, debating with God on the testing of Job's faith. Somewhere along the line however, this Satan transposed into the Satan of the New Testament, known also now as Beelzebub but then too as *Lucifer,* the fallen Angel of Light who is always trying to challenge God. He is also, rather contradictorily, known as the *Prince of Darkness.* It was once commonly thought that one could conjure up the devil merely by mentioning his name, so to avoid this danger alternative words or titles began to be used, so that, for example, "what the devil" became "what the dickens"; or instead of "the devil will..." people would say "Mr. Scratch will...". But by whatever name, he is the great tempter or seducer, offering mankind greater pleasures on Earth as an alternative to the hard road to Heavenly redemption. His price of course is an indeterminate stay for the buyer in Hell, Hades, Gehenna, all being names for the place of human torment where he resides.

Some humans who are said to have been "possessed" by the devil themselves become a party to his work. Women in this situation are known as witches, or sorceresses; men are wizards, sorcerers, or warlocks. Whilst Christianity regards witches and their ilk as part of the "anti-Christ", which is in a never-ending fight with God, elsewhere they are part of human belief which existed thousands of years before Christianity. There are biblical references, such as to Saul's visit to the Witch of Endor (1.Sam.28); executions of witches were justified by Ex.22:18 ("Thou shalt not suffer a witch to live") which became a principal justification much later for the Middle Ages crusade for burning witches. Homer referred to witches --- Medea and Circe. Hecate was the goddess of witchcraft and sorcery.

The word comes from the Old English *wicce,* a female magician or sorceress, but the idea of witchcraft is not merely not a Christian one, it is not even European. The Maoris had schools of magic, which were mainly used for good but could also be applied to less beneficial ends; the Kurumba people of South India had magic powers which were employed by others; the primitive tribes of Africa have their witch doctors; and the cult of black magic is still practised in parts of the Caribbean.

With such a long-standing and widespread history, it's hardly surprising to find witches appearing in opera too, sometimes alongside the devil (*Faust's* Walpurgis Night), sometimes on their own (*Macbeth*). Only in one two operas (*Macbeth* principally) do they have any significant influence on the plot, and always within a fairly minor role. The Devil and his side-kick Mephistopheles are, as we might expect, much more important.

There are a number of operas which have dealt with the Devil's influence on Earth, this influence usually being exerted by his aide Mephistopheles. Conflict with God often appears as a minor sub-plot, but occasionally neither the Devil nor Mephisto will appear, their presence being felt through the workings of the plot.

The Devils of Loudun by Penderecki, which is based on a real-life case of alleged witchcraft in a convent in 1634, is an example of this. Father Grandier is accused of bewitching the prioress and nuns of the Convent of St. Ursula. Jeanne, the prioress, has confessed to her priest the increasingly erotic dreams and fantasies she and her nuns are experiencing concerning Father Grandier, who is quite a handsome man. Since he is known to have a taste for women, having seduced a number of his female parishioners, it is not long before he is accused of witchcraft. He is tortured but maintains his innocence; Jeanne is exorcised (i.e. tortured). Father Grandier refuses to confess and is burned at the stake.

"The Fiery Angel"   Prokofiev, 1954

Based on a novel by Brysov which is itself based on supposedly true events in his own life, its full title is: *"The Fiery Angel; or a True story, in which is related of the Devil, not once but often appearing in the image of a Spirit of Light to a Maiden and seducing her to Various and Many Sinful Deeds, of Ungodly Practices of Magic, Alchemy, Astrology, the Cabalistical Sciences and Necromancy, of the Trial of the said Maiden under the Presidency of his Eminence the Archbishop of Trier, as well as of Encounters and discourses with the Knight and thrice Doctor Agrippa of Nettesheim, and with Doctor Faustus, as composed by an Eyewitness."* With this as a title, the opera has a lot to live up to! Fortunately it manages to do so.

Prokofiev adapted this story to tell of Renata who from childhood has had an obsession about her Guardian Angel; now, having reached puberty, her obsession has become sexual and has so angered her Angel that he has abandoned her, albeit with a promise to return in the future in human form. She meets with Count Heinrich and, believing him to be her Angel, decides to live with him, so satisfying her sexual urge for her Angel, but he too leaves her. She sets out to search for him, her Angel, but by now has become extremely unbalanced, is frequently hysterical, and continually has visions, all of which which simply proves to everyone that she is really a witch. Only one person, Ruprecht, is prepared to help her, and then only because he is in love with her.

They turn to black magic in the search for Heinrich; they acquire books on the black arts, they bring up the spirits, but are refused help by Agrippa, the expert in the subject. They find Count Heinrich, but again he rejects Renata. Angered now, she persuades Ruprecht to duel with Heinrich over her honour but just as the duel is about to start Renata sees that Heinrich is standing in a pool of light --- he *is* her Fiery Angel! She hastily tells Ruprecht that he must not harm Heinrich, but it is Ruprecht who is wounded in the duel, and quite seriously. Renata nurses him back to health, and promises herself that she will try to love him.

Having recovered, Ruprecht asks her to marry him; hysterically, she refuses, telling him that if he wants a woman he should go to a brothel! After that, even Renata realises that she needs help and enters a convent. Ruprecht meets up with Faust and Mephistopheles, who decide to look after him.

In the convent Renata's obsessive madness about her visions and her Angel have even begun to influence the nuns, and to such an extent that the Inquisition is called in. Exorcism fails; not even torture succeeds.

There is nothing left but execution, which takes place as Ruprecht, with Faust and Mephistopheles at his side, watches.

"Robert the Devil"   Meyerbeer, 1831

This is one of the few operas in which the Devil appears in person, here as a major character working his own magic without having an intermediary such as Mephisto acting for him.   Robert is the Duke of Normandy, exiled because of the evil nature of his actions.   It is the 13th century, in Sicily, where Robert's travels have led him.   He is, unknowingly, in the power of his father who is none other than the Devil himself, in human guise as Bertram, a supposed good friend.   Robert's half-sister (by his mother Alice) urges him to avoid the evil influence of Bertram but this he is quite unable to do.   Robert meanwhile loves Isabella but thanks to Bertram's influence he is disgraced and loses her.

Bertram holds an orgy with some of his demons near an old convent where there lie buried some nuns who had broken their vows.   Robert arrives and Bertram summons the nuns from their graves; they persuade Robert to take a magic bough which overhangs the grave of one of the nuns, promising him that by means of this bough all his desires will be fulfilled.   He uses the bough to gain access to Isabella in her room, but she persuades him to break it, so destroying its magic.

In the final act Bertram persuades his son to sign a contract, the price of which is his soul.   Just in time Alice arrives and manages to delay the signing until the stroke of midnight when Bertram disappears, leaving Robert free of his power.   By a magical transformation the doors of the cathedral are seen to open; Isabella is there in her wedding dress, waiting for him.

The various magical and demonic events in this work are interesting in that a number of ideas and superstitions are brought together in the one piece. The Devil's contract is obviously the same as in Goethe's "Faust" though it pre-dates the "Faust" operas; the magic bough has a long history in superstition. The scene of the nuns rising from their graves to confront Robert has its counterpart in the legend of the Wilis, young girls who have committed suicide after having been betrayed by a lover. (In the ballet *Giselle* the Wilis too come up from their graves and circle the betrayer of their latest member, dancing with him until he drops dead from exhaustion). The "magical" finale of Isabella at the cathedral highlights the ultimate triumph of good over evil.

"Der Freischütz" (The Freeshooter)   **Weber, 1821**

This tells the story of Max, a forester who must win a shooting contest if he is also to win the hand of Agathe, the Head Forester's daughter; unfortunately his latest performance in a match shows him to be well off-form. Caspar, another of the foresters, offers him an opportunity to win the contest with the use of magic bullets and arranges with Samiel, the black huntsman, to provide them. Samiel is none other than the Devil, to whom Caspar has already sold himself, and a hidden part of Caspar's deal with Max is that Samiel has agreed to the substitution of Max for Caspar. Various magical ideas are worked out, including the near death of Agathe, in the form of a dove about to be shot by the last of the seven magical bullets, but all works out well in the end with this bullet hitting Caspar instead.

But just as God makes only the occasional, and very brief direct appearance in opera --- hurling the odd thunderbolt, or playing with fire (as in the Burning Bush, or the Fiery Furnace) --- because He prefers to operate through intermediaries, so too the Devil turns up in person only very occasionally; for he has a very efficient aide, Mephistopheles, whom he uses to achieve his ends. Gounod's famous opera *Faust*, which is far and away the best of half-a-dozen works on the same subject, all based on Goethe's great poem, features Mephistopheles as its villain.

Faust

The original real 16th-century Dr. Faust was a petty player in alchemy, astrology, magic, necromancy and similar "sciences". His ideas and work became quite well known due to his extensive travels, which also spread his rather dubious reputation. His name would probably not have survived his own lifetime had it not been for the publication of the anonymous "Faustbuch", a collection of tales of the occult with reference to Faust's work which became extremely popular, was translated into many languages and went through many editions. Thanks to this book the Faust name became a byword for books on magic and the occult, which then attracted the interest of a number of poets and dramatists. Among the most notable of these was Christopher Marlowe, with his "Doctor Faustus" (1590), and best known of all, Goethe, whose "Faust" was published in two parts, the first in 1808, the second in 1838. In the period between Marlowe and Goethe, Faust's character in the literature on him metamorphosed positively from being that of a small-time charlatan to becoming a learned professor.

The Faust legend as we know it today, and specifically its adaptation to opera, derives mainly from this work of Goethe's and in particular the first part. This tells of an ageing scholar who, dissatisfied with his life and achievements, calls up the Devil for a second chance. Mephistopheles appears and in exchange for Faust's pledge of his soul, promises him what he wants --- his youth. When Faust hesitates over the price, Mephistopheles conjures up a vision of a lovely young girl. Faust signs up. He then meets and falls in love with Marguerite, the girl in the vision. He seduces her, kills her brother in a duel and is entertained by Mephistopheles at a witches' Sabbath (The Walpurgis Night). He leaves Marguerite, but later, learning that she is in prison awaiting execution for killing the child she had conceived by him, tries to save her. She refuses his offer to escape (aided by Mephistopheles) with him, preferring to die and to save her soul. This is the story that has attracted a number of opera composers.

"Faust"   Gounod, 1859

Act 1 An ageing scholar, Faust is in his study in a town in 16th-century Germany, contemplating suicide, so depressed and melancholy is he about his life. He hears the sounds of young people praising life and God, but finds their song unconvincing.

Mephistopheles appears and asks what he can do for Faust, offering him wealth, glory, power, whatever he wants. Faust replies that he wants that which contains all of these and more besides; he wants youth, which would give him back his enjoyment of pleasures, orgies, girls, everything. Mephistopheles tells him that he can provide all this, but Faust is no fool and realises that there will be a price. A price? Pooh! A mere trifle! Here on earth I will serve you, but later, down there, you will serve me; just sign here. Faust hesitates, so Mephistopheles conjures up a vision of a lovely girl, Marguerite, at her spinning wheel. See? It's simple; just sign here. Faust signs the contract, and Mephistopheles produces a potion; Faust drinks it and is transformed into an elegant young man.

Act 2 To celebrate, they go to an inn where Mephistopheles seriously alarms some of the young men with his powers. Faust meets Marguerite, but she does not accept his initial advances.

Act 3 By the garden gate to her house Marguerite sees a casket, left for her by Mephistopheles as part of his support act for Faust; she can't resist opening it and is dazzled by the jewels it contains. She has to put on the earrings, then the necklace, then the bracelet, and this leads her into the well-known "Jewel Song".

Faust, Mephistopheles, and Marguerite's neighbour Dame Marthe appear. In a comic aside, Mephistopheles distracts Marthe while Faust becomes acquainted with Marguerite, chasing after her as she leaves. They become lovers.

Act 4 Marguerite has borne Faust's baby. Valentin, Marguerite's brother, arrives, discovers her circumstances and is outraged. Meeting with Faust and Mephistopheles he demands a duel for his sister's honour. Faust takes up the challenge and with Mephistopheles' help fatally wounds Valentin, who however survives long enough to curse his sister.

She goes to pray in the church, but Mephistopheles is there too and summons his forces to meet this challenge; his demons call out to her in the church, creating confusion in her mind and preventing her from praying, until finally she hears Mephistopheles warning that hell and damnation await her; she faints.

Act 5 Mephistopheles takes Faust to the Walpurgis Night, the Witches' Sabbath. There Faust carouses with the witches and demons but suddenly sees a vision of Marguerite in a prison cell. He demands to be taken to her, and Mephistopheles, under the terms of the contract, must arrange it. They creep into the cell where she is asleep. Mephistopheles tells Faust she will be executed at dawn for the murder of her baby, and that only he (Faust) can set her free. Marguerite awakes but is delirious; recognising Faust she re-lives the happy days of their romance whilst he begs her to escape with him. But she surrenders herself instead to God, refusing Faust, and dies.

This work brought Gounod great fame, wealth and a success which he was never able to repeat. It was said to be Queen Victoria's favourite opera and is still a worldwide favourite. The elements of the story --- an old man's longing for his youth, his passion with and abandonment of a young girl, the fight for her soul between God and the Devil, together with the wonderfully melodious music, easily account for its continuing success.

8. SAINTS, AND A SINNER

*"The only difference between the saint and the sinner is that every saint
has a past and every sinner has a future"*
Oscar Wilde, from "A Woman of no Importance"

Saints appear in opera in quite considerable numbers. The idea of using
the life of a saint, or at least the events which led to sainthood, as the
hanger for an opera story has been used by many composers, and the
subject is always a Christian saint even though saints are not an
exclusively Christian concept. The concept of "saint", from "sanctus" or
"one who is holy", can be found in Buddhism (as "arhat" or one who has
attained nirvana), and in Hinduism (as "sadhu" --- the good one); even
Islam, which rejects the saintly concept, accepts the idea of the "Walid"
or "Friend of Allah". Judaism, as the "Chosen of God", or the holy
people, is in this sense an entire people of saints though the "saintly"
description would clearly only be applied to a pious and observant Jew;
however, more in context, Judaism recognises the idea of a "Tsaddik" or
righteous person, one who has lived life fully according to the Torah,
observing and fulfilling all its precepts. Jewish tradition suggests that if
there were just 38 Tsaddikim in each generation this number would be
sufficient to outweigh the sins of that entire generation, which at least
puts a value on saintliness.

It was the early Christians, around the 5th century, who began to assign
the word as a title to be given to someone who had died but whose life
was worthy of significant recall, either through martyrdom or through the
working of miracles, and who thus had a special place in heaven. But
some of the early complications in the selection of suitable Saints can be
seen in the history of St. Thais, who might be thought to have had not
one but two possible existences on Earth. Her second existence is the
one that has been recorded in opera.

Thais

Thais's first appearance was as the Athenian courtesan who, renowned for her wit and beauty, became the mistress of Alexander the Great, accompanying him on the final part of his Asian conquest. She is attributed with having persuaded him, when he was somewhat overcome with wine, to make a grand gesture and burn down Persepolis, the city now re-born as Shiraz, in Iran. (Alexander's great gifts as a leader seem to have been matched by his ability to make grand gestures; having commissioned a portrait of his then mistress Campaspe, he was so pleased with the artist's work that he kept the portrait and gave the girl to the painter as a reward). Later, after Alexander's death, Thais took up with Ptolemy, one of his top generals, as *his* mistress. In the carve-up of Alexander's empire following his death Ptolemy acquired Egypt and on his arrival there declared himself King Ptolemy I of Egypt and thus became the founder of the long and powerful Ptolemaic dynasty; Thais accompanied him there still as his mistress, but also now in the somewhat more respectable role of mother of his children; and even though he never married her, she was said to be his favourite "wife".

Around the time of the 5th century AD, when the early Church theologians were beginning to build up a roster of Saints and martyrs, they seem to have come across Thais and re-invented her, but now as a successful prostitute in Alexandria (appropriately enough, given her first incarnation), a city which at the time had a considerable reputation for the number and skills of its prostitute population. Here she was visited, according to the different versions of this story, by either Paphnutius, Serapion, or Bessision (all of who subsequently became Saints), with the intention of persuading her to repent. These visits were successful. Thais was taken with religion and, according to the story, gave away or destroyed all her possessions, left the city with whomever had worked this miracle and entered a convent where she was sealed into a cell, subsisting solely on bread and water and a prayer regime defined for her by Paphnutius (or whomever). After three years of this life she was thought to have purified herself sufficiently to be released to live with the sisters of the convent. However she died fifteen days after her release. For this act (of renunciation and penitence, not dying!), the theologians included her in their roster as Saint Thais.

This story is now generally regarded in the Church as fictitious, even though around the turn of the 20th century mummified remains were discovered in Egypt which were clearly indicated as being those of Serapion and Thais, and are now in a Paris museum, so maybe it was Serapion after all who did the deed. The Church however is not convinced that the remains, though shown with their names, are in fact who they're said to be.

The French writer Anatole France was attracted by this later story of Thais and wrote a novel around her; Massenet used this novel for his opera *Thaïs*. In the opera the priest who was supposed to have worked this phenomenal change of lifestyle upon her (now called Athanaël) is continually fighting against his erotic thoughts and dreams about her. After one such dream he succumbs to his need for her and unable any longer to resist her sublime sexuality rushes off to the convent, only to find her dying; he just has time to confess his desire for her before she dies. The opera for some reason has fallen out of the repertoire, though it was very popular at one time; it is however still remembered for its beautiful "Meditation" violin solo, which is often used as a concert piece.

Poliuto

The attractions of religion and love coming together have obvious appeal and Massenet was very good at interweaving these two themes, but his great predecessor Donizetti came up with another saintly story in his opera **Poliuto.** Poliuto, who lived in a province of the Roman empire, had become a secret convert to Christianity. Learning that his mentor had been arrested for being a secret Christian and was to be fed to the lions, Poliuto publicly declared his support by announcing that he too had become a Christian. He was also arrested, and similarly sentenced. In the opera his wife pleads with him to renounce his new faith and so save his life but he refuses to do so. She is so impressed by the power of the faith that enables him to face a terrifying death with such equanimity that she too becomes a convert and shares his fate. As a result of this display of religious certitude, Poliuto was added to the list of saints, and it was his membership there that caused censorship troubles for Donizetti for the opera has a scene, integral to the story, that shows Poliuto's conversion. The Italian censors objected to this since Poliuto had, by reason of this step, become a real saint and it was regarded as sacrilegious to portray a saint on the stage. To achieve a production therefore, Donizetti re-worked the plot, re-titled it as 'The Martyrs', and had it mounted in Paris where the censorship rules were not so stifling.

Joan of Arc

One of the best known saints was Joan of Arc, whose real-life story has attracted a number of writers, including Verdi who treated the principal events of her short life in **Giovanna d'Arco.** In this version Joan's father is fearful of her visions and voices, and believing she may be possessed by the Devil he betrays her to the English hoping that she will be burned and that her soul will thus be saved; however he soon regrets this and manages to organise her escape. Mortally wounded in a victorious battle against the English, she dies in the French camp. Oddly, given the accuracy of detail in his two early operas **Nabucco** and **I Lombardi**, Verdi seemed no longer to feel the need for similar historical accuracy here. The Church, sharing Joan's father's view that she had probably been demonised, did not interfere in her ultimate fate but the first Borgia Pope, Calixtus III, later withdrew the 'demonised' charge and declared her innocent of witchcraft and heresy. Eventually, in 1920, she was canonised.

The Carmelites

In early 1790, still in the first year of the French Revolution, religious communities were outlawed and among those affected were the nuns of the Carmelite order at Compiègne, who had to leave their Convent, adopt 'ordinary' clothes, and suffer the loss of all their possessions as well. They managed somehow to stay together and to continue surreptitiously to maintain a religious and community lifestyle. Inevitably they were discovered, imprisoned, tried for their offences, and sentenced to be guillotined. Going in the tumbrils to the place of execution, they sang hymns and the prayer for the dying, all with such calmness of demeanour that, it was reported, the onlookers and officials were all quite awed. They continued their singing as each one in turn mounted the scaffold. For the cause and manner of their deaths, they were accepted by the Church not only as religious martyrs but also, all sixteen victims, as being worthy of beatification; this whole event became the subject of **Les Dialogues des Carmélites** by Poulenc which was first presented in 1953. In the opera, the convent is sacked and the nuns expelled with a warning of their great personal danger if they continue to celebrate Mass. They take a group decision to continue to do so, except for the newest novice, Blanche, who returns to her aristocratic family. The nuns are later arrested and sentenced to be guillotined for their offence against the new atheism. As they approach the scaffold, singing hymns, they are rejoined by Blanche. The final very moving scene is of one long continuous prayer by all the nuns, the choral sound losing one voice with each drop of the guillotine.

Alexis

Possibly the most blue-blooded, at least in terms of those concerned with its conception, of all 'Saintly' operas is an early 17th-century work by Stefano Landi concerning *St. Alexis*. The idea of an opera on the life of this Saint appealed to the aristocratic Barberini brothers, who were nephews of Pope Urban VIII and the prime movers in this enterprise; one of the brothers, Francesco, was a Cardinal, and the libretto was written by the man who later became Pope Clement IX.

Alexis himself was no less well-born, being the scion of a wealthy Roman Senator; he had acquired from his parents a charitable outlook towards those less well-off than himself and developed this outlook to the point where, actually on his wedding-day, he called off the marriage to a girl from a similar background to himself, and travelled eastwards to Edessa, in Syria, which had by then become the centre of the Eastern Syrian Church, where he lived for some seventeen years in poverty. There, his holiness was eventually recognised and announced to the local population by the Virgin Mary herself through one of her images. To escape this unwanted celebrity Alexis fled back to his parents' house in Rome where his father, not recognising him, gave him a menial job and provided a corner under a staircase for him to sleep. He lived there for another seventeen years and only on his death were documents found on him giving his identity and previous history.

Even although there is no certainty concerning any aspect of Alexis' life, not even that he lived at all, this has become the substance of the story of *The Man Of God,* the description applied to him by the Virgin when she announced his presence to the inhabitants of Edessa. The story also became the subject for this early opera put together by such a distinguished group of people. The opera has almost never been performed, though it has very recently become available on CD.

Walburga

Walburga was a member of what must be one of the saintliest families in the entire roster of Saints, for not only did she become a Saint but so too did her brothers Willibald and Winebald, her father Richard, and her cousin Boniface. All came from Wimborne, in the Wessex area of England, where Walburga was educated at the monastery and where she took the veil; later, she and her brothers worked for the Church at Heidenheim, in Germany, and after her death in 779 her relics were moved, on May 1st, to a place in the Hartz Mountains. However she later became confused with Waldborg, a pre-Christian fertility goddess, and the Walburga/Waldborg confusion then became corrupted to Walpurgis; hence her association with Walpurgis Night, which takes place on the night of April 30th/May 1st when the witches gather in the Hartz mountains to celebrate their rites. It seems unfair that a member of so saintly a family should thus come to be associated with Satanic activities, but Saint Walburga has her place in the *Faust* operas.

Cecilia

Saint Cecilia of course is the Patron Saint of music and has held this honour since around the 15th century, although she actually lived centuries earlier. She was a Roman girl, brought up as a Christian, who is said to have vowed lifelong virginity, but her father felt that this was not the best lifestyle for his daughter and gave her in marriage to one Valerian. Not too disconcerted by this, Cecilia, whilst her wedding music was playing, prayed to God that He should "Make my heart and body pure that I be not confounded" and then after the wedding ceremony, in the privacy of their room she persuaded her husband to "respect my maidenhood". Succeeding in this, she went on to convert him to Christianity and followed up this double achievement of having kept her virginity and obtaining a convert by later also converting his brother Tiburtius. The two brothers became enthusiastic practitioners of their new beliefs but were martyred for their activities and are now themselves included in the rolls as Saints Valerian and Tiburtius.

Cecilia too was required to give up her missionary work but also refused so was sentenced to death; the method of execution used was to confine her to her bathroom and then to fill it with steam heated to 7 times its normal temperature; however after a day and a half of this she was quite unharmed so the order was given to behead her. Even three strikes of the headsman's axe were not sufficient to kill her and she survived for three days, which was sufficient time for her to frustrate the Senate's intent of confiscating her wealth, for she was able to make a will leaving her property to her Christian associates. For all of this she became Saint Cecilia. The reason why she eventually became the patron saint of music is supposedly because this story is included in Chaucer's *2nd Nun's Tale*, quoting her prayer before her marriage:

And while the organs made melodie
To God alone in hart sang she:
"O Lord, my soul and eek my body gye
Unwemmed, lest it confounded be".

With the particular interest centring on the point that she prayed while the music played and that her prayer was answered. Her story is the subject of the opera *Cecilia,* by Licinio Refice in 1934. Cecilia is here betrothed to Valerian and after their marriage asks him to respect her virginity. He initially refuses but his attempt at intercourse is interrupted by an Angel. Cecilia takes him to the catacombs, where he meets St. Paul and is converted. Cecilia is put to death for being a Christian but then reappears as a Saint.

Borgia, Saint and Sinner

Saint Francis Borgia gets a mention here only because his great-aunt was Lucrezia Borgia. He thus provides a lead-in to one of history's most notorious women, who is the female lead in the eponymous *Lucrezia Borgia*. Of all the sinners who ever lived on earth it is arguable that the Borgia family provided some of the greatest. In 1492 Rodrigo Borgia was elected the second Borgia Pope, having been trained to the Church by his uncle Alfonso who was then the first Borgia Pope (Calixtus III) and who as Pope, appointed Rodrigo as Cardinal at the ripe old age of 25. On his own election as Pope, Rodrigo took the name Alexander VI, and also took with him his mistress Vannazza Catanei, by whom he already had four children. Since his election to the Papacy was well after the Lateran Councils of 1123 and 1139 which stated that a priestly vocation and marriage were incompatible, and since sex was doctrinally solely for the purpose of procreation *within* marriage, and since also a Spanish Regional Council (these Borgias were from Spain) had in 306 AD decreed that all priests should abstain from sexual relations, there must have been a group act of serious sinning among the Cardinals of the day at Rodrigo's election to the Papacy. Perhaps however they were a little influenced by the heavy bribes which Rodrigo might have dispensed from the great wealth he had already accrued in the Church's service. Be that as it may, among Alexander VI's children by Vannazza --- there were others by other women but she and her offspring were his acknowledged family --- was a boy, Cesare, exceptionally talented and handsome, who was appointed by his father a Cardinal whilst still only 19. (This appointment coincided with the similar elevation of one Alexander Farnese, as a favour to the Pope's current mistress Giulia 'la bella' Farnese who was the new Cardinal's sister. Farnese later went on to become Pope Paul III and, taking his cue from his then late patron, created his two grandsons Cardinals. They were then aged 14 and 16.)

Cesare later resigned his Cardinalate in order to contract a political marriage and became a successful military commander, all the while working closely with his father on political and dynastic affairs. He still found the time however to conduct many other affairs. He also was able to arrange the murders of his brother Juan (one of whose grandchildren became Saint Francis Borgia), and of his sister Lucrezia's second husband, who had outlived his usefulness to the family. Of Rodrigo's other children by his mistress Vannazza, there was Pietro, who died young, and the daughter, Lucrezia. Lucrezia shared the drive and ambition of her father and brother Cesare but, being a woman, was somewhat constrained as to what she could do; nevertheless she readily co-operated in the family's political and dynastic plans, becoming engaged twice to Spanish aristocrats before her three marriages to Italian noblemen. Her abilities and position were such that in her father's absences from the Vatican he felt able to delegate a great deal of authority to her. Over the years she acquired a considerable reputation of her own for her treachery in the promotion of the family affairs and for the indulgence of her own personal pleasures. An example of her style was that she could organise an entertainment for All Saints Eve, given within the Vatican Palace itself, by 50 Roman courtesans (read prostitutes) for her father the Pope, her brother Cesare, herself and other members of the family.

Lucrezia's first husband Giovanni found his in-laws not to his taste and left for a safer environment, accusing Lucrezia of having an incestuous relationship with her father the Pope, who responded by annulling the marriage on the somewhat dubious grounds, given Lucrezia's reputation, of non-consummation. Her second was a victim of his father-in-law's fast-changing political alliances and barely survived an assassination attempt; whilst recovering from this he was strangled on Cesare's orders. Lucrezia was then observed with a young boy, taken to be her son, whose paternity became the subject of so much rumour that to settle the matter two Papal Bulls were issued declaring first that the boy was the illegitimate son of Cesare, then later that he was the illegitimate son of the Pope. Lucrezia, still only 22, then married for a third time, now to Alfonso, who later became Duke of Ferrara. After her father died she dropped out of politics and settled down in Ferrara where she became a significant addition to the attractions of the court; she later became drawn to a more religious way of life, and died at the relatively early age of 39. (These last two events are not thought to be connected!)

Donizetti's opera **Lucrezia Borgia** takes up her story in this third and last marriage, to the powerful Alfonso, Duke of Ferrara. He has become suspicious of her great interest in a young man, Gennaro, believing him to be an actual or potential lover. Only Lucrezia knows that Gennaro is in fact her son, whom she had arranged to have fostered out years previously. Gennaro himself knows only of a mystery mother who sent a messenger with a letter and knightly accoutrements for him; he tells Lucrezia, having no idea who she is, of his yearning for his mother. Alfonso forces Lucrezia to serve Gennaro a deadly poison, but she is able to save his life by persuading him to take an antidote. She then unknowingly includes him in a group poisoning of his friends, carried out as an act of revenge because they had identified her to Gennaro as the hated Borgia woman. Now however Gennaro, knowing her as "la Borgia", refuses to take the antidote again, preferring to die with his friends. Only as he is dying in her arms is she able to tell him that she is the mother whom he longed to know.

9.   HEAVENLY VOICES

"Opera must make people weep, shudder and die through singing..."
Bellini, to his librettist Pepoli

Of all the voice types available to humanity, quite possibly the most beautiful although certainly the most unnatural has been that of the castrati who for a long period dominated opera with their extraordinarily beautiful singing.

Castrato: *"A male singer castrated in boyhood so as to retain a soprano or alto voice."*   This usage of the word is dated by the Oxford English Dictionary to 1763, but castrati --- more commonly termed "eunuchs" --- have been recorded in history and in religion for thousands of years, and even this more limited definition of the OED, i.e. as a kind of male soprano, is pre-dated by several hundred years. Castration was variously used both as a form of punishment and, in certain ancient religions, as a kind of pre-condition for male entry to a religious life. For the Assyrians, castration was an effective, if drastic punishment; in Egypt it was the (appropriate) penalty for adultery; in Friesland (now part of the Netherlands) it was the first part of the penalty for robbery, the second part being execution. The Romans also used castration as a penalty, then banned it in the 1st century AD, but re-introduced it a couple of hundred years later. In India a Brahmin who was adulterous with his teacher's wife was offered a choice of three deaths, one of which was to amputate his penis and scrotum and, holding these severed parts in his hand, to run in a south westerly direction (this being the "direction of destruction") until he dropped dead; with this as one choice, the other two options don't bear thinking about! King Alfred the Great in England suggested the use of castration as a punishment for a male servant who raped a female servant—though he doesn't seem to have commented if the female servant was raped by her master.

Early religions were attracted to the idea of using eunuchs. The goddess Artemis, daughter of Zeus, the virgin-goddess of light (a responsibility shared with her twin brother Apollo, he having the sun and she the moon) was served not only by virgins but also by eunuchs. Her temple in Ephesus, which was one of the seven wonders of the ancient world, became one of the principal centres for early fertility cults, for Artemis had another role as the fertility goddess. Eunuchs were obviously useful as male virgins, though their part in fertility worship is difficult to see! The Syrian goddess Atalgatis (of Hierapolis, another great centre for fertility worship) was also served by eunuchs as well as virgins. Indeed there was such honour in serving Atalgatis that men would castrate themselves in religious ceremonies to qualify for this privilege and thereafter would wear only women's clothes; the castration was carried out outside the temple and the man would then run through the streets holding his bits until he found a house into which to throw them. It was then the obligation of the residents of this house to provide him with women's clothes and adornments, which he would wear for the rest of his life. Could this be the earliest recorded instance of transvestism?

Judaism comprehensively forbade the practice: "No man castrated by crushing his testicles or having his male member cut off may come into the congregation of God." Deuteronomy (23:1)

Mohammed too rejected the practice of castration saying: "He who castrates himself does not belong to my followers." This prohibition however did not seem to apply to the Islamic habit of castrating others, for there was considerable use of eunuchs within Islam as slaves and as guardians of harems and mosques (and also as court singers, as we shall see later). To supply this market young boys and men (often captured by the slave traders of Africa) were castrated and (if they survived the "operation") sold into slavery.

However Christianity did not reject castration; without positively embracing the idea there are instances of, at the very least, ambiguity about it, even in the words of Christ:

> "For there are eunuchs that were born such from their mother's womb, and there are eunuchs that were made eunuchs by men, and there are eunuchs that have made themselves eunuchs on account of the kingdom of heaven".   Matthew 19:12.

These words were the justification for some devout Christian men, as with worshippers of Atalgatis, to castrate themselves. The best known of these was Origen Adamantius, one of the principal theologians of the early Greek Church and a highly regarded scholar of Hebrew scriptures who, it is said, took these words literally and "with more zeal than wisdom, mutilated himself"; it is also said that in later life he deeply regretted his action! St. Augustine refers to "the Valesians (who) castrate both themselves and their guests, thinking that they should in this way serve God"; he does not however offer us the thoughts of the guests who were provided for in this way. Later Christian theologians have put a more acceptable interpretation on Matthew's text, taking it to mean "not gelding themselves ... but to live single that they may serve God with more freedom."

Possibly the best known of all the early Christian castrati was Peter Abelard. Living in the first part of the 12th century, he was a highly regarded teacher and student of theology whose classes and lectures were popular and well attended. Before his castration, and while in his early 30's, a good-looking man with both a very powerful intellect and a high regard for himself, he noticed among his students a young girl, Heloïse, the niece of Canon Fulbert of the Paris Cathedral. He set out on a deliberate and successful seduction, to find that in Heloïse he had met his match both in passion and intellect. She became pregnant and bore a son but neither she nor Abelard was interested in marriage; nevertheless, bowing to the anger of her uncle, the Canon, they went through a secret marriage, which Fulbert agreed not to publicise. Married life however was becoming difficult and Heloïse went to a convent where she could merge easily into the background whilst still receiving marital visits from Abelard. But hearing that his niece was now an habituée of a convent, Fulbert quite misunderstood the situation and came to believe that Abelard had abandoned her there. His anger and revenge totally changed their lives, for at his orders his men went to Abelard's quarters and brutally castrated him. The pain of this mutilation and the humiliation of the widespread knowledge of what had happened caused him to retreat from his former life.

Heloïse, now alone, took vows and later became abbess of the convent of which she had now become a member. Abelard also withdrew into monastic life, rising to become Abbot. Their story is told in *"Abelard and Heloïse"* initially through Abelard's *Historia calamitatum,* which is an astonishingly candid letter to a friend recounting his early life, his seduction of Heloïse, the castration, and subsequent misfortunes. This letter is followed by an exchange of letters between themselves and others after Abelard's *Historia* came to Heloïse's notice, and she then wrote directly to him. With these elements of youthful passion, intellectual arrogance, prejudice, misunderstanding, dramatic and tragic mutilation, plus the strong religious background running through the entire story it is quite amazing that it has never been presented as an opera. There's surely a ready-made story-line there for someone.

There is a Western attitude that eunuchs are, like the male virgins of Atalgatis, or like Origen, probably over-religious, possibly effete but otherwise harmless men whose condition takes them so far outside the pale of "normality" that they are suitable only for lowly servant-status positions such as, typically, the harem guardians of the East. However in China and the Middle East there was a very different picture. Eunuchs were of course extremely useful as guardians of the harems and women's quarters, but they could also become chamberlains to Emperors and other powerful men, and from these positions they themselves could rise to positions of considerable power and influence, becoming senior civil servants, patriarchs, even naval and army commanders. Narses, one of the Emperor Justinian's greatest generals, was a eunuch. The practice of castration, which had become quite widespread in those regions, only died out in China in 1912 with the collapse of the Chinese Empire, and in the Middle East in 1920 with the ending of the Turkish Sultanate.

In Europe however, somewhere in the 16th century, the fortunes of the eunuchs took a dramatic turn with the active move of the Church to formalise its music and this enabled eunuchs, or castrati as they were then known, to rise from their first positions as church singers and to achieve heights of fame and wealth which equated to those achieved by the most famous singers of today.

However, although the castrato singer is viewed as an essentially Italian phenomenon, which indeed he was, the Italians were by no means the first country in Europe to employ castrati as vocalists. Castrated men --- eunuchs --- had been brought to Spain during the period of the Moorish occupation in the 9th/10th centuries, as servants and harem-guardians, and some of these men showed a talent for singing which was appreciated and encouraged by their masters and provided an acceptable addition to the musical resources of the courts. When eventually the Moors were driven out of Spain, the eunuchs and their music vanished with them. It was not until some two hundred years later that the great period of castrato singing in Europe began in Italy.

Early music in Christianity was plainsong. Pope Gregory in the 6th century formalised the structure of church music and within the new discipline the Church began to develop a highly professional approach to training its choirs. Schole Cantorum, (schools of singing) were established steadily throughout Christendom, Pope Gregory himself having founded the Rome School. With these developments it became possible for choir members to have a full-time, almost life-long career in the church's musical establishment, for their training was full-time, continued over many years, and was very thorough. However, there was a basic musical problem for these choirs, a problem which had its roots embedded deeply in religious doctrine.

In the earliest days of Christianity, Paul had written:

> *"Let your women keep silence in the churches: for it is not permitted unto them to speak; ...for it is a shame for women to speak in the church."*

> 1 Corinthians (14:34-35)

With this doctrine, Paul unintentionally but quite directly contributed to the rise of castrato singing some 15 centuries later. Clearly there could be no women in church choirs, so the vocal mix available to choirmasters was restricted to men and boys. And boys presented a problem, for after a few years of training they grew up and became men, losing their characteristic pre-pubertal voice and causing the church to lose its substantial investment in their vocal training; it was, and still is, every choirmaster's headache. Efforts to cope by using the male falsetto voice were not successful, since the voice was not liked; and the boy soprano, though not being as popular as the treble, had the same problem brought on by adolescence.

The practice of castrating a boy for the sake of preserving his voice seems to have begun in Italy in the 16th century, and to have remained mainly there through the whole castrato period. The operation prevented the characteristic pubertal change in the voice and meant that as the boy developed physically he would acquire a man's physique yet retain his boy's voice, but with the consequence that, because of his now substantially enlarged lungs and diaphragm, the voice could acquire a kind of maturity that gave the castrato quite unique vocal qualities. And now, as a castrato, the boy could continue his training and career uninterrupted, to the undoubted long-term benefit of the church's choral tradition, whilst also ensuring a comfortable station in life for the castrato himself.

The operation itself (described by Heriot in *The Castrati in Opera*) was not as savage as might be thought. Basically, the child was drugged with wine, placed in a hot bath until virtually unconscious, and then the ducts leading to the testicles were severed so that in time these shrivelled and disappeared.

Not all castrati developed as male sopranos, many having the lower voice of a contralto. It has been speculated that a boy who might have developed a tenor voice instead developed a soprano voice after castration; whereas if he would have developed the lower baritone - or even bass - voice he instead became a contralto. Because of the substantially greater physical frame of the male over the female, the castrato voice had qualities which were not generally available to women, thus contributing to their huge vocal appeal.

The seemingly extraordinary vocal powers and qualities of the castrato simply cannot be appreciated today, since the last of them died some 70 years ago; the voice of only one castrato has been recorded, and that was both right at the beginning of the gramophone age and near the end of his life, and so cannot give any indication of the qualities that created so much enthusiasm over the great castrati. However, the sound-track of the film *Farinelli*, on the life of the greatest of them all, is available and perhaps gives some idea of what such a voice may have sounded like; using modern electronic wizardry, the voices of a counter-tenor and a soprano have been combined to produce a sound that is certainly intriguing, though whether it is castrato-like we can never really know.

The position of the Church in the history of the castrati has been crucial yet ambivalent. It was St. Paul's early dictum that, centuries later, established the career of castrato singers. Leading churchmen would receive approaches for financial support to enable a castration operation to be performed, against the promise that the boy concerned would join the local Schola. These approaches were usually from the parents, though occasionally from the boy himself (but probably urged by his parents), and measured against the prospect of a secure and reasonably well paid career, the sacrifice of the boy's future sexuality had its attractions. Frequently enough this financial support was forthcoming.

Yet in spite of this supportive attitude, the widespread view, both inside and outside the Church, was that castration was an unnatural and objectionable procedure. It was in 1562 that the first castrato entered the Sistine Chapel Choir; in 1589 that the Pope authorised the recruitment of castrati; in 1650 that a Schola Cantorum paid to have one of its choirboys castrated. In 1728, the papal chapel was still recruiting castrati. But by 1748 attitudes had so changed that Pope Benedict had to consider (but refused) a proposal that the Bishops should be authorised to ban castration in their Sees.

It was in this period of the mid-17th/18th centuries that the rise of the castrato coincided with a huge increase in the popularity of opera. So, not surprisingly, castrati sought and obtained opportunities in this new field. And here, in opera, was where their unique vocal qualities came to be widely heard and appreciated. There has always been a huge public preference for the high voice, and the strangely beautiful qualities of the castrati appealed enormously. It now became possible for a castrato to have more than just a long-term, secure and reasonably well-paid career with the Church; for in opera he could achieve heights of fame, wealth and adulation that paralleled the careers of top opera singers today. The most famous of all castrati, Farinelli, was for many years of his life paid substantial sums, estimated to have been around £3,000 annually, a huge amount for the time, to sing privately for King Ferdinand of Spain. Yet, as well as receiving this fame and wealth, they were also the target of great insult and vilification, which could still be overcome by the quality of their singing. A contemporary comment, concerning another very highly-regarded castrato, Tenducci, makes this point:

"At Ranelagh I heard the famous Tenducci, a thing from Italy; it looks for all the world like a man, though they say it is not. The voice, to be sure is neither man's nor woman's; but it is more melodious than either and it warbled so divinely that, while I listened, I really thought myself in Paradise".

(Tobias Smollett, author and novelist, in his book "The Expedition of Humphrey Clinker" 1771)

St Paul's dictum applied only to women in churches, and had no influence about women elsewhere; a quite different set of denigratory social values concerned women who went on the stage, either as actresses or singers. In spite of these however, women succeeded brilliantly in both activities to the undoubted benefit of their audiences. The castrati were not employed in opera to replace women; far from it, for they were much more likely to replace men. At the height of the castrato period, composers were continually producing operas with the male lead part being specifically written for a castrato voice. Many of Handel's operas, for example, were written, and cast, in this way and his audiences neither saw (nor seemingly heard) any problem with a castrato (i.e. an essentially feminine) voice coming from the throat of such eponymous heroes as "Giulio Cesare".

Today we would probably find this ridiculous and absurd, even though we have no difficulty in accepting the equivalent situation of the so-called "trouser" roles where, to provide a richer vocal mix, a male part is explicitly written for a female voice and requires the woman to dress as a man for the purpose. Romeo, in Bellini's *I Capuleti e I Montecchi* for example, Verdi's Oscar in *Un Ballo in Maschera,* Donizetti's Count Orsini in his *Lucrezia Borgia*, are all male parts sung by women, sometimes excusable where the roles are supposedly young page-boys but even there, with mature full-bosomed women in the part, visually quite silly. More intriguing however are such parts as Octavian, in *Der Rosenkavalier,* and Cherubino in *The marriage of Figaro,* where these characters are young men, written to be acted (and sung) by women, who are then required to play the part of a young man dressed as a woman!

None of these operas, nor others, raise thoughts of "how stupid, how unnatural"; we have no more problems with both seeing and hearing women in male parts than earlier generations had with hearing a womanly voice coming from a man. Because the voice was, apparently, so beautiful it was readily accepted and wildly applauded. The problem was not to do with mixing male and female elements, but simply with the means used (and the consequences to the individuals) to produce the castrato voice. It was unnatural, and this led eventually to its disappearance. Yet, having said it was unnatural, it didn't always have to be; a castrato could be a 'natural' one, the effect being simply caused by impeded or delayed physical development. If, as the boy grew through adolescence his testicles did not drop into his scrotum but remained lodged in the abdomen, his boy's voice would not undergo its characteristic change and he would develop as a "natural" castrato. There are instances of natural castrato singers, and even a well-recorded event concerning one who, straining for a high note, caused his much delayed physical development to be suddenly completed. His performance, and his career, both came to an abrupt end!

There was inevitable competition and conflict between the Church and the opera theatres concerning the services of the castrati, though not for long since the whole phenomenon of castrato singing fell away quite rapidly after the mid-18th century. When, in 1805, Napoleon Bonaparte heard Girolamo Crescentini, he was by then among the last of the great castrati. Bonaparte was so taken with Crescentini that he awarded him many honours and invited him to Paris. The last opera written explicitly for a castrato was Meyerbeer's *Il Crociato in Egitto,* in 1824 for Giovanni Velluti. Velluti (1781-1861) was effectively the last great operatic castrato, and was a man who, interestingly, had various liaisons with women during his life. After Velluti, the surviving castrati returned to and remained effectively in the area where they started - the church choirs.

When, in 1922 Alessandro Moreschi died aged 64, he was the last survivor from the period of castrato singing. Overall it had lasted 360 years from 1562 when the Papal choir in Rome accepted its first castrato singer; for perhaps 150 of these the castrati had dominated opera.

The fascination of the castrato voice has a number of components. There is, first and overwhelmingly, its sheer beauty; for even though we can never hear it now, there are more than enough very sound and well-informed opinions handed down for us to be sure that the castrato voice was indeed something very special. Then, there is its register. It was a high voice, in every way comparable to that of the soprano, the highest "normal" register for a woman, which is of course higher than a man's. The soprano is the Queen of the opera house. Even the word is indicative; "soprano" derives from "sovranno" or "sovereign" voice (the Latin "superius" or "sopressor" has the root form "sopra" or "sovra"). The soprano is the Diva (Goddess), the Prima Donna. Her male counterpart, the tenor, is not however God to her Goddess, nor King to her Queen, not even Primo Uomo, a term which has fallen out of use but is the literal male equivalent of Prima Donna. "Prima Donna" itself is a term which appears to have taken on quite specific attitudinal properties, as in "behaving like a Prima Donna" in reference to the more outrageously temperamental performances of some of opera's leading ladies ("...I suddenly became the centre of attention and that was it. That is what led to me becoming an egomaniacal monster, because that is what we opera stars are" --- Leontyne Price, opera super star), whilst its literal English translation of First Lady is now more commonly used in the theatre, or in a particular way as applied to the wife of, say, the American President.

The tenor's position in the royal hierarchy of the opera house is more akin to that of Crown Prince, and the descriptive equivalents to diva or prima donna are simply not used. No matter what his eminence, he is still 'the tenor'. And whereas the soprano has always been our Queen, the tenor has only relatively recently --- since the early 19th century --- occupied his place at her side, even as the Crown Prince. Previously this place was taken, as we have seen, by the castrato, who was indeed the King.

The tenors' occupation of the male voice supremacy as of right could almost be dated to their discovery of the "high C", the full-blooded chest note, generally first attributed to Gilbert-Louis Duprez in 1837, which confirmed the tenor as the male sex symbol and set him (almost) on a level with the soprano. Yet this high C was not at first written in by the composers. Verdi had to be asked for his permission for it to be introduced into "di quella pira" in *Il Trovatore*. Rossini, hearing it used in his *William Tell* disliked it intensely, comparing it to "the squawk of a capon with its throat cut". Nowadays it's the high C that gives the tenor much of his "sex appeal" with audiences as we wait nervously to see if he'll reach it and then applaud like mad when he does.

The high voice --- castrato, soprano, tenor --- is the one that appeals. The best parts are written for these voices and given to the heroine and to the hero (even if the male lead is not truly a "hero" but rather a romantic villain such as the Duke of Mantua in *Rigoletto*, who is a tenor because of the "romantic" bit). The operatic convention is that the heroes --- the ones "who are noble, pure and heroic and get the soprano", as Leonard Warren the American baritone observed --- are tenors.

Baritones, the next (lower) and most "normal" male voice "are the villains in opera, always the heavy, never the hero" (Leonard Warren again), but they can also be the wise good friend and counsellor to the hero (Posa in *Don Carlo* is an instance of the good friend; the eponymous *Macbeth,* of the villain). This clear depiction of baritones as the baddies however is muddied by such types as Don Giovanni, who is both hero and villain, an anti-hero perhaps, though since he comes to such a sticky end he's probably really a villain after all. The convention then follows down through to the bass voice, almost inevitably given to such characters as High Priests, Kings, Judges, etc, who show their maturity through the gravitas of the low voice.

This convention exists throughout opera; the idea seems to be that as age produces a darkening and lowering of the voice, so it also brings with it maturity, wisdom and authority so that we more readily associate these qualities with the owner of the bass voice. Even with two High Priests --- as in *Nabucco*, one each for the Babylonians and the Hebrews --- both are basses; or in *Don Carlos* with both a King and a Chief Inquisitor, both are basses. Other examples abound. Yet while this convention is almost universal for the male voice, it doesn't apply to the women. Norma, the High Priestess in the opera of that name, is a soprano whereas Adalgisa, the much younger and less senior priestess is, nowadays, the lower voiced mezzo-soprano (originally a soprano). The High Priestess in *Aida* is a soprano, and so of course is Aida herself; the wicked Amneris however, although a princess too, and one who presumably outranks Aida by virtue of being a princess of the victor nation rather than the vanquished, is a mezzo. The high/low "rule" simply doesn't apply to women; the applicable one is that the heroine will be the soprano.

The soprano is quite clearly the sovereign voice, admired as the favourite by all and the one who, to paraphrase Leonard Warren, "gets the tenor". This admiration however could get out of hand; it is recorded that having attended a performance by Jenny Lind (the "Swedish Nightingale"), at Her Majesty's Theatre in London, the London Hangman was so deeply moved that he was heard to comment 'what a throat to scrag'.

This public affection for the high voice also translates directly into more money in the pocket for the fortunate owners. This is not always appreciated by other singers. When the baritone Victor Maurel was trying to justify his demand for fees equal to those of the tenor Tamagno, he observed "When God has created the perfect idiot He says to him 'You shall be a tenor'". Toscanini shared this view, once remarking "A tenor with brains? Non posso credere!". Similarly, Sir Thomas Beecham once felt the need to supply a tenor with a little encouragement. In a rehearsal of "La Boheme", the tenor was lying on Mimi's bed:

"I can't hear you" called out Beecham:

"How do you expect me to sing my best in this position, Sir Thomas?"

"In that position, my dear fellow, I have given some of my best performances!"

Hearing of Maurel's comment Verdi remarked "So like Maurel! The baritone may be of course be a better artist than the tenor, and Maurel is infinitely more intelligent than Tamagno. But the diamond is more valuable than other stones, not because it is so beautiful, but because it is more rare." And it is more rare because the normal male voice, i.e. that possessed by the great majority of men, is baritonal. Of course this also means that the bass voice too is 'more rare', but bassi don't get paid like the tenors either. We just prefer tenors. It is the same for women;

because the normal female voice is contralto, the soprano is more rare and, being more highly appreciated, is valued more highly at the box-office. Yet if the tenor voice (with or without brains) is more rare, how do those who have it produce it to such great effect? There is a quotation attributed to Caruso who, asked just this question, is said to have replied:

"You know whatta you do when you shit?
Singing, it's the same thing, only up!"

(Quoted in H. Brown's "Whose Little Boy Are You" 1983).

10.   IDOLS

"Who could count the crowds that came that day to the Serva Padrona, of every sex, every rank, every age; they merged together tightly wedged and closely packed; a pitched battle raged in the stalls, two rivals often fighting over the same seat, each pushing the other off and hanging on, then sitting down but only half on the seat.   And like a barrel force-filled with sugar by dint of a mallet splits its sides and bursts open like a pomegranate with shattered hoops and splintered staves, that night a hundred cracks and crevices appeared in the theatre walls and woodwork, which could not withstand the pressure of so great and crazed a crush.   As soon as the angelic strains of Pergolesi, the glory of Italy, were heard, they all fell silent, straining avidly to hear, like infants at the wetnurse's breast, for that divine harmony would melt ears even harder than flint, and note by note it ravished their enraptured souls.   And then when the mellifluous voice of Tonelli stirred and intoxicated their hearts, what torrents of julep gushed from her lips and were eagerly lapped up by theirs; even the fiercest devotee of Lully hung on the fair sweet lips and, like a man with his arms around his naked mistress, was lost to the world."

This extract from a review of a performance of *La Serva Padrona,* a new work by Pergolesi being given in Naples in 1733, offers scope for speculation.   Making allowances for Italian temperament, operatic enthusiasms, journalistic hyperbole, etc this review still seems to describe a situation that is unlikely to be encountered anywhere else than in an opera house, perhaps the only sort of place in the civilised world other than a revivalist religious meeting that can generate such passion, such intense emotion that moves people so far outside their normal behaviour patterns in experiencing and expressing their appreciation of a particular performance.   What is it, in opera, that creates this effect?   Is it the music? The singers? The drama? The production? Or the whole thing, that is greater than the sum of its parts?

Seen as a play with music, opera draws greater crowds (and applause) than a play, so clearly the music is very important. Yet whilst concerts of classical music, particularly those featuring the opera "pops", draw the crowds, they don't produce the appreciation the way opera itself does. The best singers can by themselves draw huge crowds. The "Three Tenors" phenomenon is one example; "Pavarotti in the Park" is another.

The singers are clearly something special, yet who in his right mind pays through the nose to see and hear a grossly overweight tenor of middle age, with very limited acting ability, trying to impersonate an ardent and romantic young man? Or, for that matter, an overweight soprano of uncertain years in the part of the sexy, voluptuous young woman who has lit the fires of desire in the tenor? Since it is clearly neither the age nor the physique of the singers nor, with a few notable exceptions, their histrionic ability that "turns people on" so, the only thing left is the voice. But we can usually hear the voice "in the flesh" so to speak at concerts for a lot less money than an opera ticket would cost (the three tenors concerts excepted); or, disembodied, for far less money on extremely good records. So it has to be the total opera-house experience that creates the effect. And in support of this simple conclusion there is the applause phenomenon: an audience of normal, civilised adults at a concert might, in extremis, give the orchestra and/or the soloist a 5 or even 10-minute ovation; but this same audience might give an opera performance, and in particular its star singers, as much as 50-minutes of applause (Vienna 1989, Ricciarelli & Domingo in *Otello*).

In a concert the audience listens to the entire piece, all movements, before expressing an opinion of the performance, remaining silent even in the pauses between the movements; whereas in the opera-house each aria or chorus is an occasion to interrupt with immediate enthusiastic applause. Why? What happens to audiences in an opera-house? Why these different styles of behaviour? One answer clearly is that in opera it is not the music but the singing that is the occasion for the interruption; in *Traviata* for example the popular overtures to Acts 1 and 3 are usually only lightly applauded, whereas all the arias receive the full weight of audience approval. By contrast, some years ago at a concert in Ely cathedral where Menuhin and Kentner were playing Beethoven sonatas, there was a magical ambience which combined with the music and the performance in such a way that at the end of the concert there was complete silence: everyone was quite literally entranced, spellbound. Only slowly did a ragged clapping gradually build up into a full-scale appreciation which lasted for several minutes. But in an opera-house, no matter where it is, no matter how dramatic or moving the story and the performances have been, there is instant applause, with some people not even waiting for the curtain to fall; there is competition (or so it seems) to be the first on one's feet shouting 'Brava'. The only comparable situations are on a ballet stage or, a "pop" concert audience of teen-agers (usually girls) worshipping their favourites. The young Sinatra and his teeny-bopper fans are in this sense no different from the mature Domingo and his equally mature fans.

Perhaps a more appropriate analogy is that of revivalist Christian ministers, and the huge audiences they attract with their messages of future salvation that succeed in whipping-up their audiences into totally emotional, unthinking worship. For that surely is what we can observe in opera: worship, worship of the star singers, the Idols, the Deities of opera who tour the world visiting the temples set up to their worship on a continuing basis rather in the manner of the Hindu gods. And their followers make their devotions in these huge temples, to the background of the "ecclesiastical" music of Verdi, Puccini, Rossini, etc. It is surely not coincidence, rather it has to be evidence of some kind of divinity that all the "three tenors" for example appear to have defied their human status in at least one respect, since even well into middle age they appear to have not one grey hair between them! And why else would we refer to the reigning queen of any opera house as the Diva unless we were acknowledging her divinity too? Perhaps opera has indeed become its own religion.

A real-life idol from an earlier age, at least to the very many society women who so adored him, was the Sicilian composer Vincenzo Bellini. Very good-looking, though in a feminine rather than a masculine way, he seemed to have been touched by the gods themselves in the favours heaped on him. Musically he was highly gifted; he played the piano very well by the time he was five years old, and had composed his first piece of music at the age of six. He did not have to wait for public recognition of his intensely melodic operas, he had great personal charm, his music was exactly right for his time, so unsurprisingly he became a national idol in Italy. He had many affairs with women, including a long-running affair with a married lady. Even men would fall under his spell: "His figure was like his melodies...graceful, appealing, fascinating..." Not everyone loved him however; he was famously described by one (male) writer as "...a sigh in dancing-pumps"; he was not particularly admired by many of his professional colleagues either for he could be very bitchy when he chose. He died at the early age of 33, to the desolation of his female admirers and the greater loss to opera at large.

The opera idol who, for me, epitomises the *Prima Donna* image was Nellie Melba. Born Nellie Mitchell, in 1861 in Melbourne, she was briefly known as Nellie Armstrong following a failed marriage. When her teacher in Paris, Mme Marchesi, insisted that "Armstrong" was not an appropriate stage name, the future Prima Donna tried for a name reminiscent of her native Melbourne, eventually coming up with "Melba", a name which gained Madame's immediate approval. As a star, she travelled in huge style; the Pullman Company in America supplied her with her own coach which had "Melba" in large gold-painted letters on each side and came complete with its own personal staff; in hotels she demanded only the finest, softest linens; at Covent Garden she was the only singer who was given her own dressing room, not to be used by anyone else. Responding to a poor practical joke, she demanded that the entire staff of Covent Garden be instantly dismissed, and the manager felt he had to obey her wishes (Melba in a fury could terrify anyone), but re-engaged them all the next day. She could not easily accept anyone on stage whose presence might draw attention away from her; the rising star Titta Ruffo gave a brilliant performance at a Covent Garden dress rehearsal, in the name part of *Rigoletto*, with Melba as Gilda, and the next day found he had been replaced; Melba thought he looked too young to play her father! (Some years later, when she offered to sing Ophelia opposite his Hamlet in Naples, he sent a note declining the offer; he said he thought she was too old for the part). Again at Covent Garden, she refused to allow the new young tenor John McCormack to share in the final applause: "In this House, nobody takes bows with Melba".

She was a tough bargainer, demanding outrageously high fees and, in the end, getting them. She was cautious about getting her voice onto the new medium of records, but when she did, her commercial nous was right there up front; knowing that Caruso's records were priced at £1, her contract insisted that hers were to sell for a guinea (£1:05 in today's money). But she could be remarkably generous; when a good friend commented, on a particularly cold day, on the advantages of her Rolls Royce she insisted on giving it to him. Some quality about her extracted special tributes, such as the two, possibly the most famous of their kind, when leading chefs created special dishes for and gave them her name: who has not heard of *Peach Melba*, or *Toast Melba*? Yet her voice, gorgeous though it was, does not seem to have been of the stuff that would create the conditions for such huge popularity as she enjoyed; it was more like a boy's voice, as she herself acknowledged when she commented "My voice is like a glorified boy's voice." Or as on another occasion when, at a service in Chartres Cathedral she remarked to a friend "I hate these boys. At thirteen they are doing what it took me years to do. And I don't know that they're not doing it better." But what a voice it must have been to have drawn such huge admiration and praise over such a long period (she was at the top of her profession for some 35 years, virtually her entire working life). Opera houses around the world demanded her, and even the most sceptical (originally) such as La Scala, whose audience didn't get to hear her until she had already earned world-wide fame --- and what can that be worth, the Milanese audience would ask, without *our* approval? --- even they acknowledged her supremacy when eventually she appeared before them. She knew what she had, vocally, and exploited her talent ruthlessly and arrogantly. Even at 60, asked when she might retire, she said "There is no Anno Domini in art. I have the voice of a genius...why shouldn't I sing for a thousand years?" She didn't of course, dying in 1931, just two months before her 70th birthday, after retiring at age 65. It is a woman such as this who, more than anyone, puts me in mind of the comment that "The difference between a prima donna and a piranha, is that one of them uses lipstick."

A contemporary of Melba's was Enrico Caruso, who showed his own touch of genius for his timing in the matter of when to be born; this was quite superb, for he grew to be a young man just beginning to make a name for himself when the gramophone was invented. A London business, The Gramophone and Typewriter Company, had one of their scouts, Fred Gaisberg, in Milan looking for talent; he heard Caruso and immediately arranged a deal with him for ten recordings, to be made in one session, at an inclusive fee of £100. He wired details to London, only to receive the reply: "Fee exorbitant, forbid you to record". Fortunately, he read this with his equivalent of Nelson's blind eye and went ahead with the recording anyway, and the rest is history. It is said of the consequences of this piece of far-sightedness of Gaisberg's that "the gramophone made Caruso, and Caruso made the gramophone". Of his voice, Nellie Melba, who in spite of her Prima Donna attitudes was well able to recognise and acknowledge her equals and who had a legendary stage partnership with him, said "...his was the most wonderful tenor I have ever heard. It rolled out like an organ. It had a magnificent ease, and a truly golden richness". To go with his voice, he had a quirky sense of humour that was often let loose on stage; partnering Melba in *La Bohème*, and reaching the aria "Che gelida manina..." ("How cold your hand is! Let me warm it for you..."), he placed a hot sausage in it!

Caruso travelled the world's opera houses, attracting colossal enthusiasm wherever he appeared, and in spite of the huge media attention he attracted his popularity was seemingly untouched (perhaps it was enhanced) by his well-documented womanising. In Milan, in a breach of promise case, the Judge referred to his "morally deplorable act"; an American actress noted in her memoirs that he "he made love and ate spaghetti with equal skill and no inhibitions"; he was even once arrested in New York, charged (and convicted) with molesting a woman. Born to working-class parents in Naples, he was the first of a large number of his mother's children (supposedly eighteen) to survive past infancy. He died in 1921 at the tragically early age of 48, of peritonitis, leaving an incomparable legacy of his recorded work, and a name as *the* tenor of the 20th century. Even Melba did not achieve the equivalent title for herself.

Possibly the greatest idol of our own time (including all of the "three tenors") was Maria Callas, perhaps now even more of a legend than she was an idol in her lifetime. She was a singer who was adored by the public, a woman who could engage in high-profile confrontations with colleagues, whether rival sopranos, or conductors, other singers, even opera house general managers. She had a fiery temper, was extremely volatile emotionally, made very poor choices of the men in her private life, and was able in mid-career to transform herself physically from a fat, plain woman with a glorious voice into an extraordinarily attractive and elegant woman with a glorious voice. But in opera she was not just a voice; she was a singing-actress *par excellence* who was yet more than that, for even when she spoke her words she brought intensity of expression to new heights on an opera stage. On stage she was magnetic, yet even though her voice later developed a notoriously ugly wobble which she seemed quite unable to deal with, she never allowed it to affect either her choice of roles or her acting. She developed two great stage partnerships; the first with Tito Gobbi, the wonderful Italian baritone --- their 1964 *Tosca* performance at Covent Garden is the very stuff of memory; and then with the tenor Giuseppe di Stefano, which regretfully they tried to continue well after both should have permanently retired from singing. She died in Paris in 1978 at the age of 54.

11.   CANTORS, SHMANTORS

Having been born into an orthodox Jewish family and brought up, at least in our early years, in a religiously observant environment, my brothers and I became proper "Shabbat Shul-goers", going regularly to the Sabbath service every Saturday morning. My two abiding memories of those days are first of longing for the moment when, with the Torah Scroll replaced in the Ark, the Rabbi would step out onto his pulpit and stand patient and silent for a few moments before addressing the congregation with his sermon for the day; for this was the time when we kids were given temporary leave of absence to let off steam outside since we were regarded as being too young to benefit from the Rabbi's wisdom. (Of course, after one's Barmitzvah at 13, one was now a man and had to stay in and listen; many of us weren't convinced that the Barmitzvah presents were sufficient compensation.)   Second was the sheer pleasure of listening to some of the prayers and psalms being sung by our Chazan (Cantor) who, when he was in full voice produced a beautiful sound that together with the familiar melodies would fill the large synagogue with what seemed like heavenly music.

In Orthodox synagogues the congregation is led in prayer by the Cantor (or Chazan, in Hebrew) who sings or chants the entire service. Not surprisingly these men (exclusively men) are selected for the quality of their voices and singing ability as much as for their religious vocation, and their training has as much to do with singing as with the religious aspect of their work. From this training a cantor learns particular vocal capabilities which are not necessarily shared by, or even known to many opera singers, for the demands on the cantor's voice can be immense. Not only must he sing for the best part of 2 or 3 hours, with few rests, during a normal Sabbath service; but on High Holy days he is required to perform for many more hours. This special expertise and technique of cantors is often studied by opera singers; Caruso, for example, would whenever possible attend synagogue services so that he could study the unique vocal methods of cantors.

Yet even with a strong tradition of cantorial singing, there have been relatively few Jewish singers in opera compared with the Jewish presence in other sides of musical expression. In Europe the Church had a long established basic principle that for any Church office the holder had to have been baptised. This of course was perfectly reasonable and proper, but the power and influence of the Church extended it as a requirement almost throughout the continent to encompass almost any official position anywhere. The politically fragmented map of 18th/19th-century Europe, with Princes, Dukes, Electors and the rest ruling little city states, usually under the "protection" of, or as part of, the Holy Roman Empire, made such a development quite straightforward. These minor rulers, exercising their own extensive powers of patronage, awarded positions such as, e.g., Court Musician, Kapellmeister and so on to those who found favour with them and their friends. Talent was not a pre-requisite for these posts, though obviously it helped. And by virtue of the baptismal rule, Jews were totally excluded. Things changed only slowly, but by the 19th century the rise of influential composers such as Meyerbeer, Halévy, Mendelssohn, Offenbach and others showed that these changes were occurring, though mainly in the more liberal, enlightened environment of post-Napoleonic Paris, and that where there was exceptional talent, exceptions could be made. Yet, even as late as 1897, such an exceptionally talented a person as Gustav Mahler found that before he could secure the appointment of Director of the Vienna Opera he had to undergo baptism and become a Catholic.

Jewish singers found that with the very many very good baptised singers available, they had to be quite outstanding to be heard. And, since most of the good male Jewish singers became cantors (it was virtually the only opportunity they had to express their talent) they then found that their own cantorial culture operated against them, for it was felt very strongly to be the antithesis of cantorial/synagogal art to "profane" it on the stage. For instance one famous cantor, Baruch Schorr, extended his musical talent to writing an operetta, *Samson* which was presented at the Yiddish Theatre in Lemberg, the town where he was Principal Cantor at the main synagogue. When the time arrived for curtain calls his audience, who were of course to a large extent also his congregants, were so shocked to see him actually on the stage with his leading lady that he was officially suspended from his duties for a month! (Schorr was so cross about this that he soon after took up an appointment as Cantor at a synagogue in New York, where he stayed for five years before responding to pleas from his former congregants and returning to Lemberg. His son, Friedrich Schorr, later developed a fine career particularly in Wagnerian opera, and sang for many years at the Berlin State Opera until the arrival of Hitler).

Another 19th-century Cantor who similarly entered his name in opera through his son, was Isaac Judah Eberst. Eberst made his living in part as an itinerant musician and in part as a Cantor in any of the synagogues in the towns where he was playing. Coming from a small town near Frankfurt called Offenbach, he became known as "der Offenbacher", a name which he soon adopted as his own. His children were all very musical, but one, Jacques, built a great international career for himself in Paris, as a composer of operas and operettas which have never left the world-wide repertory.

In other fields of musical expression, such artistes as Heifetz, Menuhin, Perlman, Zukerman, Stern --- to name but a few --- would probably enter most people's lists of the world's greatest violin players; Rubinstein,

Schnabel, Horowitz, Moiseivitch, Barenboim and so on would similarly figure in any league of the all-time great pianists. And all of these are Jews. Yet in spite (or perhaps because) of the cantorial culture there is no such list of Jewish opera singers. Great Jewish opera singers there have been: Tucker, Peerce, Kipnis, Jadlowker, Beverly Sills ...and that's about it. But even Tucker was no Caruso (or Gigli, or Domingo). Among the women the story is the same; Beverly Sills for example was a very popular opera singer, primarily in New York, but could not reach out to the wider public in the way that say, Callas or Sutherland or Ponselle have done.

Thanks to Jewish Law and practice women have had even less opportunity than men. They faced the same baptismal barrier; the field of cantorial singing was simply not open to them; their role in Jewish life required them to take the responsibility for providing the essential requirements of a Jewish home, with all its intricate needs; and there was of course the external pressure that simply impugned the reputation of any woman who appeared on the stage. No wonder there were no Jewish female opera singers (Pauline Lucca excepted).

Nevertheless, in the 20th century there have been a number of very good cantors who have made the jump from the synagogue *bima* (dais) to the opera stage. These include:

Richard Tucker (1913-1975). Born Reuben Ticker, he was a great American tenor who started his singing career in the synagogue, becoming the Principal Cantor at one of New York's most prominent Temples (synagogues). Tucker became one of the 'greats' at the New York Metropolitan Opera; Rudolf Bing, the Met's famous General Manager (and also Jewish) has recorded that he planned for Tucker to become the House tenor, which for many years he did. Tucker remarked that in one sense there was no real difference between cantorial and opera singing: "They both demand blood and guts." He was so highly regarded by the Met and its patrons that when he died in 1975 they paid him the unique tribute of holding his funeral service on its stage.

Jan Peerce (1904-1984). Born Jacob Pincus Perelmuth, he, like Tucker, was a prominent Cantor in New York who became a world famous opera singer. He said of his cantorial work: "One should be able to sing hours and hours without fatigue. Cantorial work is a marathon and you shouldn't get tired". Peerce and Tucker became brothers-in-law when Tucker married Peerce's sister.

Robert Merrill (1917-   ) wanted right at the outset to be an opera singer but needed to earn money both to live and to fund his studies. Under the name of Merril Miller he would assist in synagogues, particularly on Yom Kippur and Rosh Hashanah (New Year) services.

Josef Rosenblatt was the Cantor with the Chevzedek congregation in New York (one of the city's largest) and had a recording contract with Columbia Records which led to world-wide fame. However his religious principles stood in the way of any development of an operatic career, and he turned down an offer of $2000 an evening (this was in 1917!) to appear as Eléazar in *La Juive* with the Chicago Opera. He also refused a very substantial sum to sing 'Kol Nidrei' (a sacred chant near the start of the 25-hour Yom Kippur Service) in the very first talking-film *The Jazz Singer* about the son of a cantor who wished to sing popular music rather than follow his father as a cantor.

Herman Jadlowker started his singing career in a synagogue choir in Riga. Later he moved into opera, singing at the Berlin State Opera and the Vienna State Opera. Then he went to Tel Aviv, where he became a cantor (thus reversing the "usual" sequence), and a teacher of voice.

Moshe Koussevitzky until his death (in 1966) was widely regarded as the finest cantor in the world. As a young man he trained and became Cantor at leading synagogues in Poland and Lithuania whilst at the same time developing an operatic career. He was taken by the Nazis and sent to the infamous Treblinka concentration camp; however he was rescued and arrived in Russia where he had great success in the opera houses of Moscow, Leningrad and many provincial cities. He was awarded the Stalin Order of Merit for his contribution in raising the morale of the Russian people during the war. Afterwards, he settled in America where he both gave concerts and was the cantor at the Temple Beth-El in Brooklyn. He was one of four brothers, all of whom were famous cantors, though Moshe was the only one to move into opera. One of his brothers, David, was the cantor at the Hendon synagogue, in North West London, from 1937-1951, where I heard him. He went on to the Temple Emanuel in Brooklyn, becoming a neighbour of Moshe.

Now, the situation has been transformed for both men and women. The twin arrivals of radio and records combined to rapidly promote the fame and wealth of singers of all types, specifically here including cantors. Oddly, this development has created a strange echo of the Castrato phenomenon, for just as the Church lost its best castrati to the greater commercial opportunities offered by the rising popularity of opera, so today good cantors are often attracted to the greater opportunities available in opera or in other equally commercial areas. The film *The Jazz Singer* brilliantly illustrates this. Cantorial art has lost its inhibitions about appearing on stage, and some very good cantors have consequently been lost to the synagogues.

12. DID YOU REALLY DO THAT, GOD?

1. One of Caruso's first important roles was as Rodolfo in a production of *La Boheme* at Livorno, near Puccini's home. As a relative unknown, it was written into his contract that he must first audition for and gain the approval of Puccini himself. After hearing him sing, Puccini turned to Caruso and asked "Who sent you to me - God?"

2. After a performance by Rosa Ponselle (possibly the greatest soprano of the 20th century) there was the following exchange between Lotte Lehman, and Geraldine Farrar (both of them also very great sopranos):

> *"How is it possible to have a voice like hers?"*

> *"Only by special arrangements with the Lord!"*

3. *"How do you think of these lovely melodies?"*

"God, madame, sent me down some of his angels, and they whisper sweet melodies into my ear".   Gounod, to an admirer.

4. Sir Neville Cardus, writing on Mozart's *Magic Flute*, said:

"This opera is the only one in existence that might conceivably have been composed by God."

The Magic Flute

If this opera had indeed been composed by God, He perhaps might have felt, not merely that Mozart was the only person who could be used as a conduit for its introduction, but that this accreditation should never extend to any later works, for this was Mozart's last opera; he died some 8 weeks after its first performance, in Vienna in 1791. In the light of Sir Neville Cardus's speculation, these two events, following so close together and in the same year, caused me to wonder whether there might have been any other happenings that would indicate 1791 as a special year, thus possibly giving some support to Sir Neville. There were of course many events then that would have given particular pleasure to various sections of humanity; for instance, Vermont joined the United States, Haydn wrote his *Surprise* Symphony, the Marquis de Sade wrote *Justine*; all very interesting, but not really up to *The Magic Flute*'s stature in terms of the universal pleasure given to the human race. Only one thing comes close to (some might say exceeds) it. For it was in 1791 that Mme. Marie-Fontaine Harel, a farmer's wife in France, invented Camembert cheese. There has been no suggestion hitherto that the hand of God might have been detected here, but it did happen in the same year as *The Flute*. 1791 *was* a special year, and perhaps there's more to Sir Neville's speculation than is immediately obvious.

Mozart and his librettist Schikaneder were both freemasons, and freemasonry had recently been outlawed in Austria; Empress Maria-Theresa even employed armed forces to shut down the lodges. So Mozart and Schikaneder saw their new work as an opportunity to respond to that situation by deliberately presenting a masonic ritual on stage.

The practice of Freemasonry in its present form is about 400 years old, having developed out of the practices of the craft of masonry from which it takes its name. The craft went into a steady decline at the end of the great cathedral-building period in England in the late Middle Ages, and a number of lodges started accepting non-working members in order to sustain their finances. From a decision in the early 18th century when four London lodges, each with its own Master and complement of non-working members, decided to associate together as a "Grand Lodge" with a single "Grand Master", the movement grew quickly and has now become an international association of independent lodges and Grand Lodges, modelled on this United Kingdom original. From this small beginning grew modern freemasonry, which now has very little to do with its craft origins. And with this change came the adoption of many of the rites and symbolisms of the even older orders of chivalry and religion that are now an important part of freemasonry association.

There are two basic requirements for membership: first, a belief in a "Universal Architect", a God, a Supreme Being, or whatever title might be used, but without there being any requirement to worship this Being in a particular way; and second, to be male. This freedom of belief has appealed equally to (male) members of all religions, yet it has also given rise to denunciations of un-Godliness by fundamentalist religious groups. Since freemasonry does not call, for instance, for a belief in the Messianic nature of Christ's mission, nor a belief in the essential truths of the Torah (nor, for that matter, of the Koran, nor any other "Holy Book", which possibly explains the virtual non-existence of freemasonry in militant Islamic countries), it has become a focus for opposition from a number of religions.

Partly because of the secrecy of much of the masonic rituals, partly because of what is perceived to be a lot of ritualistic mumbo-jumbo (at best); and partly, in western countries, because of its exclusion of women, there is also a lot of prejudice towards freemasons, at least some of which may also be due to supposed individual lodge prejudices against certain religious or ethnic groups. The movement is thought to be strongest in countries that have, or have had links to the United Kingdom where it all started, but it is also well represented in Europe, South America, and Israel.

In spite however of the relatively recent nature of freemasonry, its philosophical roots are claimed to go back more than 3000 years; for instance, one of the significant symbols in freemasonry is the "Pillars of Solomon's Temple", which form one of the most important elements of masonic imagery. Other concepts and symbols are traced back to the Egyptian civilisation; Act 2 of *The Magic Flute* has an Egyptian setting.

"Die Zauberflöte" (*The Magic Flute*). **Mozart, 1791**

The action takes place in an undefined place at an indeterminate time. *Act 1* Tamino, a prince from another country, is trying to escape from a huge snake; as he passes out in terror three young Ladies appear and kill it. Although they would prefer to stay and admire the handsome stranger, duty requires that they report his appearance to their Queen, the Queen of the Night. Enter Papageno, a strange character dressed as a bird, who straightaway introduces himself in the popular aria "Der Vogelfanger bin ich ja" ("I am the birdcatcher"). Tamino wakes, and Papageno claims to have killed the snake, but when the three Ladies reappear they padlock his mouth for telling such a lie. They also show Tamino a portrait of the Queen's daughter Pamina, with whom he instantly falls in love.

He is taken to see the Queen of the Night; she tells him, in *"O zittre nicht"* ("Oh! Tremble not"), that Pamina has been kidnapped and is held captive by a demon named Sarastro; she promises Pamina to Tamino if he will rescue her. For the rescue mission Tamino is given a magic flute; Papageno, who is released from his padlock and ordered to accompany him, is given some magic bells; and three boys are provided, who will guide them to the princess.

In an Egyptian room Pamina is being threatened with rape by Monostatos, a Moor who has her in his control. Papageno wanders in and they frighten each other on sight --- a birdman and a black man. Monostatos exits, leaving Papageno to tell Pamina that Tamino loves her and will rescue her; this news is sufficient to cause her immediately to fall in love with Tamino.

Tamino, led by the three boys, has arrived at a place where there are three temples, from one of which an aged priest emerges. The priest succeeds in cleansing Tamino's mind of his hatred for Sarastro, no demon after all, but a wise ruler who has ultimate power over Pamina. Tamino plays his magic flute, bringing all the animals out to listen; Pamina and Papageno rush through, trying to escape, but are recaptured by Monostatos. Papageno plays his magic bells, enchanting Monostatos and all the slaves. Sarastro arrives in a chariot and orders that Pamina and Tamino, who have now met for the first time, be taken to the Temple of Examination.

Act 2 Another Egyptian scene, this time with pyramids. Sarastro and his priests agree that Tamino should submit himself for examination for admission to the brotherhood. Sarastro informs the priests that the gods have decided that Tamino will marry Pamina. Everyone sings the hymn *"O Isis und Osiris"*.

In a temple court Tamino and Papageno are led in. Tamino has decided to undergo the tests, the first of which is to remain silent; Papageno's interests are first to deal with his acute hunger and thirst problem, and then to find Papagena, the woman of his dreams. The three Ladies appear, trying to win them back to the Queen's side.

Pamina meanwhile is asleep in a garden, being lewdly watched by Monostatos, who runs off at the appearance of the Queen of the Night. She orders her daughter to kill Sarastro. The Queen leaves, and Monostatos returns, to continue propositioning Pamina who is now rescued by the appearance of Sarastro.

Papageno breaks the rule of silence by talking to an old woman who tells him that she is really just 18 years (and two minutes) old, that she has a sweetheart called Papageno, and that her name is... but there is a clap of thunder and she disappears. Pamina is distraught because Tamino will not speak to her. Sarastro tells them they will be separated but will meet again. Papageno finally gets the glass of wine he's been longing for; the old woman reappears and Papageno promises to marry her when he learns that if he doesn't he'll be imprisoned for ever. She instantly turns into Papagena but again immediately vanishes. In a setting with a volcano and a waterfall, Tamino's final trial awaits him. He is told that he will be purified by fire, water, air and earth and, if he overcomes his fear of death, he will have proved his fitness for the mysteries of Isis. Guided by Pamina, and playing his magic flute, he passes the test.

Papageno is now desperate to find Papagena and has to be reminded by the three boys of his magic bells. As he plays them, Papagena comes to him, this time to stay. The Queen and her Ladies, with Monostatos, attack the temple but are driven off by storms. Night vanishes, the sun emerges, and Sarastro receives Tamino and Pamina.

PART 2. GREEK MYTHOLOGY AND LEGENDS

The Greek and the Norse legends have been a major source of inspiration for composers and their librettists. Opera is shorthand for sex, murder, passion and jealousy, and nowhere is this more clearly seen than in the way these old myths, and particularly the Greek ones, have fitted into the opera genre so comfortably. The great plays and poetry of Homer, Sophocles and Euripides have been used by composers from Monteverdi in the 17th century to Richard Strauss in the 20th for some of their finest work. The jealousies, anger and lusts of the gods mirrored those of their human charges, the kings, queens and citizens of the many island countries and mainland states that then made up Greece. Practically all human emotion is here in these mythic tales, brought vividly to the opera-house stages of the world in dozens of operas written over the centuries.

One opera, unfortunately now lost, which thoroughly mixed the godly and human elements was Gilbert and Sullivan's *Thespis, or, the gods grown old* which, in 1871, was the first of their many collaborations. Preceding the involvement of Richard D'Oyly Carte, this first G&S work was the result of behind the scenes activity by John Hollingshead, Manager of the Gaiety Theatre and "licensed dealer in legs, short skirts, French adaptation,...", in bringing them together. The theme concerns the ageing Olympians, who are finding everything too much for them; even the Temple on Mount Olympus is a ruin. A touring company of human actors arrives, and the gods devise a plan to swap places with them. Act 2 has the actors happily playing the gods, but getting everything in a muddle; "Apollo" has to help "Diana" at night, for instance, so the sun is shining then. The volume of complaints from the humans down below forces the gods to take back their responsibilities. Because of poor production arrangements the opera was a failure; and Sullivan's music has been lost, though Gilbert's lyrics survive.

The Myths

Most of the legends have a number of variations and the early Greek writers seemed to choose whichever one best suited the work they were creating; the composers who wrote many hundreds of years later similarly did not feel obliged to stay with all the literary detail from which they were working, and also selected versions of the legends to suit themselves. There is generally no single accepted "authorised" version of any of them so the outlines given below do not necessarily conform with those perhaps more familiar to some readers, or even used by the opera composers themselves. A point to keep in mind about the relationships of the various gods and demi-gods to each other is that, because they were immortal, their offspring did not necessarily have the same obvious relationships to each other. For instance, Zeus fathered Apollo and also the Muses, yet the Muses were not necessarily "conventional" sisters (or half-sisters) to Apollo since they were born not just of different mothers but at a much later time.

13.   ORPHEUS

Orpheus was the mortal son of Apollo and the Muse Calliope (the Muse of eloquence and epic poetry), who with her eight Muse sisters was among the daughters of Zeus.   (In some versions he is the son of Oeagras, the King of Thrace and Calliope, and received his lyre from Apollo himself).   Apollo, a son of Zeus (and twin to Artemis), and a principal god among the Olympians, included music and the harp among his many responsibilities.   With such parentage and family background it's not surprising that Orpheus grew up to compose beautiful songs; he also played them very sweetly with his lyre and sang them with a remarkably attractive voice.   The overall combination was of such magic that it was said that even the animals danced to his sounds.

Returning from his adventure with Jason and the Argonauts, he fell in love with and married the beautiful nymph Eurydice; on her wedding-day she was in the fields when, trying to escape from the would-be rapist Aristeus, she trod on a snake and died from its bite.   Heartbroken, Orpheus gained permission from the gods to travel to the underworld to see if somehow he might be able to bring her back to the everyday world. As he travelled the frightening journey down, his pleas for permission to continue, framed in songs, charmed all the guardians along the route to the underworld; even Hades, the King of the Underworld, and brother of Zeus, was sufficiently moved to allow Orpheus to take Eurydice with him on his return to his own world.   However Hades made one condition, that on their return journey neither of them must look back; if either did so, Eurydice would not complete her journey.   Within sight of the surface, Orpheus glanced back to check that Eurydice was still following, and she instantly disappeared, forever.

Wandering aimlessly and alone, he met up after a few months with a group of Maenads, priestesses of the god Dionysus; Orpheus declined an invitation to join their celebration of the god, on the not unreasonable grounds that he preferred to worship Apollo. In a fury they attacked him, tearing him limb from limb; his head, accompanied by his lyre, floated away to the Island of Lesbos, still calling out for Eurydice. The fragments of his body were collected by the Muses and buried at Olympus. Later, on Lesbos, an Oracle of Orpheus was established which gradually acquired considerable renown.

Dionysus had other names but he is probably best known as Bacchus, the god of wine; his priestesses, the Maenads, were otherwise known as the Bacchantes, whose celebrations usually took the form of wild, naked, drunken dancing. The event of Orpheus' death having been so directly bound up with the worship of Dionysus, the Orpheus legend later became entangled with the cult of Dionysus, and the religious philosophy of Orphism developed around him and his by now sacred poems. By the $5^{th}/6^{th}$ century BC the cult of Orphism had become established to the level where there were many travelling priests expounding its principles, many of which will be familiar. For instance, Orphism held that man has a dual nature, being both divine and evil; that sin exists and has to be atoned for; that man has an immortal soul which passes on at the moment of death; that there is a need for an ascetic purity which (among other things) prohibits sex other than for procreation.

Orpheus' attempted rescue of Eurydice is the story that has attracted dozens of composers; three have famously given it operatic treatment. Monteverdi wrote **Orfeo** in 1607, basically following the well-known legend; then Gluck, also putting a very straight interpretation on the story, produced a masterwork, **Orpheus and Eurydice** that contains some quite ravishingly beautiful numbers. About a hundred years or so later came Offenbach, the German Jew whose **Orpheus in the Underworld** was his own masterpiece, a hugely entertaining work which even has the gods of Olympus doing the can-can in the Underworld.

"Orpheus and Eurydice"   Gluck, 1762

Eurydice, beloved wife of Orpheus, is dead. Orpheus and some nymphs are mourning around her tomb. He resolves, with encouragement from the god of love, to attempt to bring her back. As he approaches the Underworld, the Furies and the terrifying watchdog Cerberus refuse him passage but his songs of explanation for his journey arouse sufficient compassion for them to allow him to proceed. He arrives in Elysium, where again his pleas are successful and Eurydice appears. Leading the way back to the surface but forbidden to look back at her, Orpheus has to release her hand; Eurydice soon accuses him of coldness towards her and complains that death is preferable to life with such a person as she perceives Orpheus to have become. Her complaints become unbearable and, as Orpheus instinctively turns round to reassure her, she dies. His aria "Che faro senza Euridice..." ("what shall I do without Eurydice...") is out-standingly the finest number in the entire opera. He determines to kill himself to be with her but is saved by the appearance of the god of love; Eurydice is revived again and they are reunited on Earth.

"Orpheus in the Underworld"   Offenbach, 1858

The marriage of Orpheus and Eurydice has reached the stage where they can't stand each other, and Eurydice particularly can't stand Orpheus' awful violin playing. She has been having an affair with a shepherd who, unknown to her, is actually the god Pluto. Orpheus wants to get rid of her and does a deal with Pluto, who puts a poisonous snake in the fields; it bites Eurydice and she dies, happy to be released from the hell of her marriage; the underworld will be heaven by comparison. Orpheus is happy at the way things have turned out but is compelled by Public Opinion to set out on a rescue mission. He travels to Olympus to ask Jupiter to help in the return of his wife; it turns out that the gods there are all pretty bored and fed-up and Jupiter sees Orpheus' request as a great opportunity to deal with an incipient revolt; he decides they will all go with Orpheus to the Underworld.

There, Jupiter himself falls for Eurydice, but at a bacchanalian party where the gods all dance the can-can, he has to let Orpheus take Eurydice back to Earth, providing he doesn't turn round on the way. On their way back, Jupiter throws a thunderbolt, Orpheus turns round to see what happened, Eurydice drops dead again and has to remain there as a bacchante, to the great relief of all concerned.

14.   THE TROJAN WAR

The Trojan War was for a long time thought to be the very stuff of legends; a mythical fight around a mythical place by a people of myths. But in the second half of the 19th century the site of ancient Troy was discovered in Asia Minor, near the mouth of the Dardanelles; subsequent excavations established that there had been several cities (Troy I-VII) on the site, with evidence of heavy fighting over a period from 1193-1184 BC, a timespan that would fit with the 10-year duration of the war with the Greeks.

Although there are many more Greek than Trojan characters featuring in the legends and the operas, the Trojans of this time have their share of literary and operatic fame. Queen Hecuba of Troy gave her husband King Priam many children, most notable of whom was Hector, the eldest son and greatest warrior, who led the fight against the Greeks. Paris, the second son, whose seduction of Helen was the trigger that started the war, was second in valour only to Hector, and was the avenger of Hector's death at the hands of Achilles. Paris killed Achilles with an arrow, guided by Apollo, to Achilles' only vulnerable spot, the heel by which he had been held by his mother Neris, the sea-nymph, when she immersed him as a baby in the river Styx to give him protection against otherwise mortal injury.

The next best known of Priam and Hecuba's children who had a part to play in the war is Cassandra. She was a beautiful young woman who was desired by Apollo; he bribed her with the gift of prophecy so that she would sleep with him but, having received his gift, she refused to deliver on her bargain; Apollo's revenge was to modify his gift so that her prophecies would never be believed. (In a variation of this story Apollo offered to settle for a kiss, and when Cassandra refused even this he spat into her mouth, with the curse that no-one would believe her prophecies.) The most significant consequence of this episode was that although Cassandra continuously and correctly foretold of doom and disaster to the Trojans, no-one ever believed her and she was at one stage even locked up as a raving madwoman. Later, urgently counselling against taking possession of the huge wooden horse left behind by the apparently departing Greeks, she was still not taken seriously. In the event, Troy fell and Cassandra tried to hide in the temple of Athene, where she was found and raped by Ajax. This was not only rough on Cassandra, it also proved to be unfortunate for Ajax since the temples, like latter-day churches, were regarded as holy sanctuaries; the gods arranged for his early death in retribution for this sacrilege. His rape of Cassandra was not the issue; where it occurred was what offended the gods. In the victorious share-out among the Greeks of spoils and captives, Cassandra became the property of Agamemnon, the Greeks' overall leader; he made her his slave, forced her into a sexual relationship as a result of which she bore twins, and took her back with him to his palace at Mycenae. Arguably, it was her cavalier treatment of Apollo that was, next to Paris's act of seduction, the most significant cause of the destruction of Troy, since had her prophecies been believed Troy might not have fallen.

The last of Priam's children to feature in these Trojan War operas was Troilus, who loved Cressida, daughter of a renegade Trojan priest; after three happy years together, Cressida ran off with the Greek prince Diomede. Troilus was killed when he came looking for revenge.

"The Trojans"   Berlioz, 1863

This is a long 5-act opera which is usually presented either in two parts, or as two separate operas in the form that Berlioz himself used, the first being *The taking of Troy* and the second *The Trojans at Carthage*.

Act 1 is outside the walls of the city near the deserted Greek camp. The Trojans are deeply curious about the huge wooden horse left there by the Greeks when they took to their ships and sailed away. Many believe this to be an offering to the goddess Athene, but Cassandra can see into the truth behind the horse and warns against her father's plan to take it inside the walls; she foretells the destruction of Troy if the horse is brought in, but her prophecy is ignored.

Act 2 is in a room in Aeneas' palace. (He is the son of the Trojan Prince Anchises by the goddess Aphrodite, of whom Poseidon foretold that he would rule over the survivors of the fall of Troy.) He is also a brave warrior and cousin of Hector, whose ghost appears to him; he must escape, take with him as much Trojan wealth as possible, and found a new city of Troy by the river Tiber in Italy. The Greeks emerge from the horse and, with the element of surprise easily overcome the defenders, but call out that Aeneas has escaped, taking the city's treasure with him. In Priam's palace women pray, while Cassandra prophesies that Aeneas will found a new Troy; however now that her betrothed is dead she herself would rather die than be taken by the Greeks. She stabs herself, and those women who feel the same way also kill themselves.

Act 3 is in Carthage, ruled by Queen Dido. Dido was formerly Elissa, daughter of the King of Tyre; her brother had murdered her husband Acerbus in order to seize his wealth and property, forcing her to flee to

Libya where she founded the city of Carthage (its remaining ruins now a suburb of Tunis) and became its Queen. She re-named herself *Dido*, meaning "wanderer".

For all her outward denials she knows inwardly that her sister's view that she should re-marry is appealing. News arrives of ships driven ashore for protection from the storms; Ascanius, son of Aeneas, appears with gifts for the ruler of this country. Learning that Carthage is under threat from its neighbours, Aeneas offers his help and leads both Trojans and Carthaginians to victory against Queen Dido's foes.

Act 4 starts with the well-known "Royal hunt and storm" in a forest near Carthage. Hunting horns herald the arrival of the hunting party, but when a storm breaks Dido and Aeneas become separated from the others and shelter in a cave where they affirm and consummate their love. Later in the evening in Dido's garden there is much discussion of the Dido/Aeneas relationship, and a celebration of Aeneas' recent victory. He tells Dido that Hector's widow Andromache has married Pyrrhus, the son of Achilles, the man who killed her husband. This news somehow soothes her concerns over marrying again after her husband had been murdered. She and Aeneas again exchange vows of love, but Mercury, the messenger of the gods, appears and reminds Aeneas of his duty to go to Italy.

Act 5 is at the harbour of Carthage where the Trojans are getting ready to leave. Aeneas knows he must go but is wracked by his love for Dido. She appears; she is distraught and alternately pleads with him to stay and curses him for leaving. But all her words are useless, for the Trojans, with Aeneas, are bound by fate to leave. From a room in her palace

Dido watches the fleet set sail and orders a great fire to be built on which she will burn everything that reminds her of Aeneas; she also decides to die. Outside by the pyre Dido ascends to its top and prophesies the future arrival of a great soldier, Hannibal, who will avenge her on the descendants of Aeneas. She then shocks everyone by stabbing herself with Aeneas' sword and as she dies her final vision is of Rome.

"Dido and Aeneas"   Purcell, 1689

Act 1 is in Carthage where Aeneas is welcomed by Dido when his fleet shelters in the harbour from the strong winds. Her growing feelings for him are approved by her close friend Belinda as a welcome relief from her worries.

Act 2 A Sorceress has sent for some witches to help her in plotting Dido's downfall; Dido *"whom we hate as we do all in prosp'rous state"* is to be mentally destroyed by ensuring that Aeneas does not stay a day longer than they can help. The Sorceress will deceive Aeneas into leaving Dido by sending him a false message reminding him that his destiny is at Rome, whilst the witches will blow up a storm to spoil the wedding nuptials of Dido and Aeneas. The next scene is in the grove where Dido and Aeneas consummated their love the night before; a storm blows up, everyone runs for cover except Aeneas who is called upon by Jove's messenger "Mercury", the Sorceress in disguise, reminding him that he must go to Italy, and that he must leave immediately. He is fooled by "Mercury" and knows he must obey. He sorrows for Dido: "One night, enjoy'd; the next, forsook" but puts the blame for his desertion of her on the gods.

Act 3 is by the harbour where the Trojans are preparing to set sail. Dido learns that Aeneas is preparing to leave and confronts him; he offers to stay, but then decides he must leave. Dido realises that she cannot live without him and knows that she will die, for her heart is broken; she sings her famous lament "When I am laid in earth", and dies.

Helen of Troy

When Zeus selected Paris to be the judge in a heavenly beauty contest he surely couldn't have known what he was starting. The goddesses Hera, Athene, and Aphrodite coveted the prize of a golden apple, inscribed "to the fairest" but none was prepared to submit her charms to an honest contest. Hera offered Paris wealth and power if he chose her; Athene offered him wisdom and victory in war; Aphrodite promised him possession of the most beautiful woman in the world. The whole subsequent history of the Trojan War shows how much he should have chosen the wisdom offered by Athene, for he gave the apple to Aphrodite and thus set in motion the events that led up to the Trojan War.

Soon after this beauty contest Paris was sent by his father on a mission to Sparta; whilst there in the Court of King Menelaus, and with the active help of Aphrodite, he seduced Menelaus' beautiful wife Helen and persuaded her to elope with him to Troy. Helen, nominated by Aphrodite herself as the most beautiful woman in the world, had had no ordinary conception. She was, according to one legend, the daughter of the goddess Nemesis who herself had been seduced by no less a being than Zeus; trying to escape his attentions she changed herself into a goose but Zeus became a swan and achieved his desire. Alternatively she was

Zeus' daughter by Leda, then Queen of Sparta, whom Zeus had lusted after; he changed himself into a giant swan, swooped down upon her and raped her. On the evening of this same day Leda also received her husband Tyndareus (who in another variant of these legends was also her father) and the complex result of this double love-making produced four children. These were Helen, Clytemnestra (who herself features prominently in these legends), and Castor and Pollux whom Zeus later elevated to stellar status. The birth process itself was unusual since in this version Leda bore two large eggs; one contained Helen and Pollux who were Zeus' children, and the other Clytemnestra and Castor, who were Tyndareus'. Clytemnestra was thus Helen's half-sister.

Helen's many would-be husbands included Odysseus, Theseus and all the Island Kings and Princes except Agamemnon, King of Argos, who was already married to Clytemnestra. All were taken by her great beauty, but she chose Menelaus, who later became King of Sparta and who was the brother of Agamemnon. With the onset of the Trojan War a whole new set of consequences, stories and legends were set in motion, many of which are still celebrated in the opera houses of the world today. Just one of these consequences is that, by her seduction and elopement, Queen Helen of Sparta is forever remembered not by this, her legitimate title, but instead as the beautiful Helen of Troy, "the face that launched a thousand ships", who is also the central figure in a very entertaining comic opera.

"La Belle Hélène"   Offenbach, 1864

Queen Helen, somewhat less than happy in her marriage, hears about a beauty contest involving an apple and a handsome shepherd, who of course turns out to be Paris in disguise, and who has been promised by Venus (Aphrodite) the love of the most beautiful woman in the world. Helen's husband, King Menelaus, is tricked into taking a journey to Crete, so Paris grabs the opportunity of slipping into Helen's boudoir disguised as a slave. Surprisingly, Menelaus enters and discovers them in bed but Helen tells him it's his own fault since if he'd only gone to Crete as he was supposed to have done he wouldn't have discovered them. Paris discreetly exits. Later, while Menelaus and Helen are down on a holiday beach, a priest arrives to tell Helen she has to make a journey with him to atone for her sins; once on board ship she is delighted to find that the priest is none other than Paris in yet another diguise, and the Trojan war scenario is set.

"Paride ed Elena" *(Paris and Helen)*   Gluck, 1770

Paris arrives in Sparta in pursuit of Helen, acknowledged as the most beautiful woman in the world; he calls in an IOU from Venus (Aphrodite) whom he had chosen as the most beautiful of the goddesses, and also enlists the help of Cupid, Aphrodite's son by Adonis. Helen resists his attentions and becomes more nervous of him as the urgency of his wooing increases. When Cupid tells her that soon Paris and his fellow Trojans will be leaving, she acknowledges her true feeling for Paris and takes off with him for Troy. Athene appears, warning of the destruction of Troy.

"Troilus and Cressida"   Walton, 1954

Troilus, a son of King Priam, is in love with Cressida, daughter of the priest Calkas who is preparing to defect to the Greeks. Cressida meets Troilus in the home of her uncle Pandarus where they declare their mutual love and spend the night together. The Greek Prince, Diomede, appears; he immediately falls for the beautiful Cressida and lets it be known that her father Calkas will only be allowed in the Greek camp if he is accompanied by his daughter, but that she can later be ransomed by the Trojans. Cressida agrees to go with her father and Troilus determines to raise the ransom as quickly as possible.

In the Greek camp Cressida is without news of Troilus, because all his letters have been intercepted by her maid Evadne; Calkas wants to encourage a match with Diomede and thus closer ties with the Greeks, so he has enlisted Evadne's help in isolating Cressida from Troilus. Believing Troilus has abandoned her, Cressida has become susceptible to the attentions of the handsome Diomede and agrees to marry him, being encouraged in this change of affections by both her maid and her father. Troilus and Pandarus enter the Greek camp under a truce, with news that Cressida will soon be able to return to Troy, as the ransom demand has been raised. They see Cressida when she enters in her wedding dress; Troilus immediately claims her as his, while Diomede demands that she rejects Troilus, which she refuses to do. Troilus reveals, to Diomede's dismay, that he and Cressida have previously spent a night together. Calkas tries to resolve the situation by stabbing Troilus in the back and is instantly seized by Diomede and thrown into chains, to be returned to the Trojans. Diomede then also orders that Cressida, whom he now regards as no better than a whore, must remain, now to be available for the pleasure of the Greek troops. With this sentence upon her, Cressida picks up Troilus' sword and kills herself.

15.   THE AGAMEMNONS

The Greek forces gathered by King Menelaus to recover Helen were led by his brother Agamemnon, King of Argos. When the fleet of about 1000 ships had assembled at Aulis, a port on the south-eastern seaboard of Greece noted for its temple to Artemis, Agamemnon relaxed with a recreational hunt which resulted in the killing of a stag sacred to Artemis. Absolutely furious, she promptly prevented any movement of the fleet by the simple manoeuvre of stopping the winds, and before she would enable the departure for Troy demanded from Agamemnon an equivalent penalty, the sacrifice of his fairest daughter Iphigenia. There was no softening her fury and Agamemnon was forced to agree to her demand simply in order for the fleet to be able to leave Aulis. On the pretext of marrying her to the great warrior Achilles, he sent for Iphigenia who duly arrived with her mother Clytemnestra, Agamemnon's wife. Both were understandably upset to learn the real cause of their journey but neither was in a position to make any effective protest. Iphigenia surrendered herself for sacrifice but, just before the knife struck Artemis relented, spirited her away in a cloud (to Taurus where, in due course, she became one of Artemis' priestesses) and substituted an animal for the sacrifice. The Greeks were then able to leave and start the Trojan War in earnest.

Clytemnestra was not amused by seeing what she believed was her husband's callous sacrifice of their daughter, and her views about him underwent a fundamental shift. While Agamemnon was away she took up with his cousin Aegisthus as her lover, and on Agamemnon's eventual return accompanied by Cassandra, the captured Trojan princess who was now his slave and mistress, Clytemnestra and Aegisthus murdered him in his bath on his first night back. They also killed Cassandra and her twin babies by Agamemnon, and then ruled at Mycenae together for several years. Ironically, as they neared his home Agamemnon had been more and more urgently warned by Cassandra of their impending doom, but of course he did not believe her. (If only she had honoured her deal with Apollo ...)

Apart from Iphigenia, Agamemnon and Clytemnestra had three other children; daughters Chrysothemis and Electra, and a son Orestes. At the time of their father's murder Orestes was still small and, fearing for his life, his sister Electra smuggled him away and herself began to nurture a deep hatred towards her mother. A few years later Orestes, now a grown man, returned with his friend Pylades, and with Electra's active encouragement took revenge for their father's death by murdering first his mother and then her lover Aegisthus.

Orestes ordinarily would have been allowed by the gods to avenge his father's murder by killing Aegisthus; however the murder of his mother as well, even though she was a full partner in the killing of her husband, ranked as the forbidden sin of matricide and called for retribution; this was a crime for which Orestes was subsequently tried (and ultimately acquitted) by the gods. In trying to atone for his matricide Orestes, with Pylades, travelled to Taurus in search of a statue of Artemis to present in expiation of his sin. However, the custom and practice in Taurus at the time was that all travellers who arrived there were sacrificed to Artemis; Orestes and Pylades were captured and made ready for sacrifice. Iphigenia, Orestes' sister and now Artemis' priestess there, later recognised Orestes, freed him and Pylades, helped them to remove the statue of Artemis from the temple, and then fled with them to Attica, where she established a new temple dedicated to Artemis.

This is a family in which the father is intent on sacrificing one of his daughters before going off to war; the girl's mother later murders her husband and his mistress on their return; their son (actively encouraged by another of his sisters) in turn murders both his mother and her lover; and then later himself comes close to being sacrificed by another of his sisters. Unsurprisingly it has proved an attractive source for a significant amount of Greek drama, which in turn has supplied the inspiration for a great many operas.

"Iphigenia in Aulis" Gluck, 1774

Effectively trapped in Aulis by unfavourable winds, Agamemnon is persuaded that a significant sacrifice is needed to soothe the anger of Diana (Artemis) and decides to send for his daughter Iphigenia, inducing her to come to Aulis by telling her that she is to marry Achilles. Regretting this plan and trying to put off this terrible act of sacrifice, he tells her on her arrival that Achilles has changed his mind about the marriage, and that she must go home, but Achilles arrives to disprove this story. She learns the real reason for her being in Aulis, and for the sake of her father and for the Greeks decides to submit. The King orders the sacrifice to go ahead, yet again regrets his decision. The sacrificial pyre is prepared, Achilles rushes in with his men to prevent the sacrifice, the pyre suddenly bursts into flames as Diana relents, and burns itself out. Favourable winds suddenly blow up and a satisfactory ending is achieved.

"Iphigenia in Taurus"   Gluck, 1779

Iphigenia, now a priestess of Artemis on the Island of Taurus, has a nightmare; it is about the deaths of her parents and seems to forecast that she will be responsible for the death by sacrifice of her brother. Two strangers appear, forced onshore by the winds, and tradition calls for their sacrifice; they are Orestes, driven by the Furies to atone for his murder of his mother, and his friend Pylades. He can atone by recovering the statue of Artemis, which has been profaned on Taurus by human sacrifice.

Imprisoned, Orestes is questioned by Iphigenia, but brother and sister do not recognise each other even though she feels a strong affinity towards him. She decides that one of the captives will be freed to take back a message to her sister Electra, in Sparta; the remaining captive will be sacrificed according to tradition. Orestes determines to be the sacrifice, saying that he deserves to die, and Pylades agrees to be the messenger. On the sacrificial altar, at the moment when the priestess's knife is poised over him to strike the death blow, Orestes sighs with what he thought would be his last breath "thus died my sister at Aulis". Iphigenia's hand is stopped; she recognises her brother and halts the sacrifice. The people are aroused in protest and attack both Iphigenia and Orestes but they are saved by the return of Pylades with his fellow Greek sailors. In conclusion Artemis then affirms that her altar must never again be stained by human sacrifice.

"Electra"   Richard Strauss, 1916

Electra is desperately unhappy in the court of Clytemnestra and her lover Aegisthus, losing all interest in her own appearance. Chrysothemis, her younger sister, tells her that Aegisthus and Clytemnestra plan to have her locked up; Electra tries to enlist her help in a plan to kill their mother and her lover but Chrysothemis only responds with her yearning for a husband and family of her own. Clytemnestra appears and asks Electra what she can do to stop the terrible nightmares she's having. Electra tells her mother that a sacrificial victim is needed, and that it should be Clytemnestra herself. She then goes on to tell her mother that anyway she (Electra) doesn't believe all the rumours that Orestes is dead.

In the evening, hearing from Chrysothemis that Orestes is indeed alive, Electra tries unsuccessfully to persuade her sister to help in killing their mother and her lover. Realising then that if anything is to be done she must do it herself, she starts to dig for the axe used to kill Agamemnon and which is now buried in the courtyard. A stranger approaches; it is Orestes and after some misunderstandings he and Electra recognise each other and she powerfully tells him what he has to do. He goes into the palace; Clytemnestra dies with loud screams which attract Aegisthus into the courtyard to find out what's happening. Coolly, Electra lights some torches to help him find his way into the palace. At the sound of his cries for help, Electra begins a wild dance and collapses as it climaxes. Orestes rushes out, now pursued by the Furies.

Odysseus

Odysseus, also called Ulysses, was outstandingly the wiliest of all the Greek leaders; it was his plan to withdraw and leave behind the giant wooden horse. His long journey home to Ithaca after the final destruction of Troy is recounted in Homer's *Odyssey*, and many of his adventures have been written into operatic history. There have been a number of operas on the subject of his encounter with the sorceress Circe; she had turned his sailors into swine, but Odysseus had been provided with protection by the gods against being similarly converted and was able to compel her to restore his men to their proper form. Realising that as an enchantress her magic had no effect on him, Circe turned on her womanly charms, against which Odysseus found he had no defences, so she was able to keep him with her on her island for a year. On his eventual return home he killed, with the help of his son Telemachus, the many suitors trying to persuade his wife Penelope that her husband was dead and that she should marry one of them. Telemachus himself later visited Circe's island and according to the legends married her or (in another variation) her daughter. Although on this episode alone, the return of Odysseus, there have been many operas, just one survives: *Pénélope*, by Fauré, and even this is rarely performed. Telemachus does not appear in this work, and Odysseus's slaughter of the suitors is carried out with the assistance of local shepherds and their butchering knives.

16.   IDOMENEUS, MEDEA, THESEUS

Idomeneus was King of Crete, one of the many Kings who took part in the war to win back Helen. Following its successful conclusion he and his ship, within sight of home, were caught up in a huge storm; desperate for salvation he prayed to Neptune, promising to sacrifice to him the first male person he would meet on land if their lives would be spared. The storm died down, everyone survived and Idomeneus, walking along the sea-shore, met a young stranger. It had been many years since he had left Crete for the war, so it was understandable that he did not recognise his son Idamantes or that the young man did not recognise his father, for he had been a small child when Idomeneus had left for Troy. Idamantes was at this time in love with Princess Ilia, one of the daughters of King Priam of Troy, who had been captured and sent back to Crete and who was secretly in love with him. Also present was Princess Electra, who had gone to Crete for a while to escape the unpleasantness at home and who also loved Idamantes but with an unrequited and very jealous love. So this was the situation faced by Idomeneus on his return; a son whom he had unwittingly sworn to sacrifice to Neptune, the same son who had the love of two women, one a Trojan prisoner, the other the passionate and embittered victim of circumstances. And this was the scenario of Mozart's *Idomeneo.*

"Idomeneo"   Mozart, 1781

The opening scenes bring the action forward to where Idomeneo is faced with the price he has to pay for his rash prayer to Neptune for a safe landing. In his palace he decides to send his son away with Electra to Argos, for his own safety. Electra of course is delighted, but Ilia is distraught and admits to Idomeneo her love for his son. At the harbour, where Electra joins Idamante and Idomeneo at their parting, the departure is halted by a great storm and a fearsome monster, both blown up by Neptune who is furious that Idomeneo has dishonoured his promise. Idomeneo offers himself as the sacrifice to Neptune, who is not placated, and the storm continues to rage, causing terror among the population.

Back in the palace Ilia sings of her love for Idamante; he appears, promising to kill the monster or die trying and this noble sentiment causes Ilia to tell him too that she loves him. Idomeneo urges his son to leave but is warned that the people are demanding action and are threatening a revolt. In the public square he tells them the terrible truth, that the sacrificial victim must be his own son Idamante, and receives their sympathy at his position. But there is no way out and the sacrifice preparations are put in hand even as Idamante returns having slain the monster.

He recognises his father's difficulty and submits himself to the sacrifice. As Idomeneo's sword is raised, Ilia rushes in begging to be the sacrifice; after all, as a Trojan she is an enemy of the Greeks and so should be the one to die. Even Neptune's heart is softened by these two selfless acts and he relents provided Idomeneo abdicates. The Oracle announces that Idamante and Ilia will reign together in Crete and everyone except

Electra is happy; she despairs at the way things have turned out for her and rushes off.

Medea

Medea was the daughter of King Aetes, Guardian of the Golden Fleece; she was also something of an enchantress, with a viciously cruel streak to her character. Aphrodite had been helping Jason in his search for the Fleece and as part of this support, when the Argonauts arrived at Aetes' island she caused Medea to fall hopelessly in love with him so that she would provide whatever help might be necessary in the final stage of the quest for the Fleece. The lovesick Medea promised to help Jason overcome all her father's obstacles and gain the Fleece if he would marry her. Jason readily agreed and, using magical aids provided by Medea, he succeeded in gaining the Fleece.

Fleeing from the fury of her father, who suspected Medea of helping Jason, they escaped taking with them her young brother. However her father's pursuit was gaining on them so Medea delayed him by the simple but effective device of killing her brother and throwing him, piece by piece, in their father's way, correctly calculating that he would slow down in order to pick up these pieces. After a successful escape, which included a stay on her aunt Circe's island, Medea and Jason settled in Corinth where they married and she bore him two sons. Some ten years later however Jason left her for the daughter of King Creon of Corinth, thus initiating one of the most savage acts of revenge ever recorded about a woman. Pretending to accept the situation, Medea gave to the new bride a poisoned wedding dress which caused the wearer to die in agony once it had been put on; she killed King Creon by giving him the gift of a new crown to be worn at the wedding, which burst into flames on the wearer's head; and then murdered her two sons by Jason, knowing how much he loved them.

After the murders Medea fled from Corinth to Athens, having received a promise of sanctuary from King Aegeus, Theseus' father. One version of the legend has her later married to Aegeus, but afterwards being thrown out of Athens for her repeated attempts to murder Theseus. According to Herodotus she finally settled in Asia in the territory that later became known historically as the country of the Medes. This great story is the stuff of tragic opera and various parts of it have been the subject of several operas, the best-known being Cherubini's *Medea* which essentially re-tells the legend, with minor differences.

Theseus

Every nine years, a group of seven young men and seven young girls had to be sent from Athens to Crete in tribute to the powerful King Minos of Crete; they were sacrifices to the monstrous half-man half-bull, the Minotaur which lived in the labyrinth of Minos' Palace at Knossos. Minos was the son of Zeus by Europe, sister of the king of Thebes. Europe was a direct descendant of both Zeus and Poseidon, so when Minos boasted of his Olympian connections he was telling the truth and once, in response to a direct challenge on this, he asked Poseidon to send a white bull, which he promised to sacrifice to the god. All challenges were silenced when a magnificent snow-white bull walked ashore from the sea. However when Minos saw this marvellous animal he decided to keep it and to sacrifice instead a much inferior creature. In anger at this insult Poseidon caused Pasiphae, Minos' wife, to conceive an immense lust for the white bull and to want to mate with it. To achieve this desire she turned to Minos' famed architect Daedalus, who constructed a lifesize wooden cow, covered it in cowhide, and fitted a door in the back for Pasiphae to enter and position herself inside its hollow back legs. The Minotaur was the result of the mating. After this demonstration of the power of Poseidon's revenge, Minos dared not kill the monstrous creature and ordered Daedalus to build a huge labyrinth underneath the palace which would contain the Minotaur in a maze of passages so complex that the creature could never find its way out.

Theseus, son of King Aegeus of Athens, volunteered to be one of the Athenian tributes, intent on killing the Minotaur; Ariadne, a daughter of King Minos, fell in love with him on sight and gave him an immensely long thread to trail behind him so that he would later be able to find his way out of the labyrinth. Having killed the beast and found his way back to Ariadne, they became lovers and Theseus escaped with her to Naxos, where he subsequently abandoned her. According to the various versions of the story, Ariadne then hanged herself, or died in Cyprus, or was found by the god Dionysus (Bacchus), who married her.

"Ariadne auf Naxos" (Ariadne on Naxos)   R. Strauss, 1912

Prologue: At the residence of one of the wealthiest men in Vienna final plans are in hand for the entertainments at the banquet to be given that evening. There is to be a new opera, *Ariadne auf Naxos* given by the Composer, a student of the Music Master; there will also be a Harlequin singing and dancing group; and a great fireworks display which is to commence promptly at 9 o'clock. A final rehearsal for the opera is held up because the violinists are at dinner, Ariadne is not around, and Bacchus doesn't like his wig. The Composer is further irritated when he's told that the good-looking girl he's spotted is Zerbinetta, the lead singer for the rival Harlequins. However he's again distracted, this time by an idea for another new tune for his opera. Further chaos ensues when it is announced that, to ensure the fireworks start promptly at nine, both preceding entertainments will be given simultaneously, with the Harlequins interspersing scenes with the opera. Zerbinetta, hearing about the plot of *Ariadne,* scorns the idea of languishing in sorrow; "get another lover", is her approach.

The Entertainment: Ariadne is asleep on Naxos; the three nymphs watching over her, Naiad, Dryad and Echo, sympathise that she is able to think only of Theseus who has so cruelly abandoned her, and of her longing for death. She awakes but, still in a dreamlike state, is hardly aware of the appearance of Zerbinetta and the Harlequin quartet, who comment on her state. Zerbinetta tries to tell Ariadne that she's not the only woman to have been abandoned by her lover and won't be the last; she offers her own philosophy (i.e. find another lover), but Ariadne is inconsolable. The three nymphs re-appear, excited about the news of the arrival of the handsome young god Bacchus, fresh from Circe's charms. At their meeting Ariadne mistakes him for a returning Theseus, whilst he mistakes her for Circe in another form; as they sing together they become aware of their errors, and Ariadne's yearning for death changes to a longing for love with Bacchus. They engage in a passionate embrace and disappear into her cave. Zerbinetta is pleased that things turned out the way she would have wished.

"Ariane"   Massenet, 1906

Theseus' gratitude for Ariadne's help in the slaying of the Minotaur extends to asking her to return with him to Athens as his Queen, accompanied by her sister Phaedra. Whilst the three of them are stranded on Naxos, Phaedra, who is also in love with Theseus, manages to gain some of his interest but of course this considerably disturbs her sister. Phaedra prays to Adonis for help but his statue topples over and kills her.

Ariadne is distraught at the turn of events and successfully pleads with Persephone in the Underworld for her sister's return, only to find then that Theseus does actually prefer Phaedra. He leaves Naxos with Phaedra, and Ariadne is drowned.

"Phaedra"   Pizzetti, 1915

Theseus has succeeded his father and is King of Athens with Phaedra as his wife. She has fallen in love with her stepson Hippolytus, Theseus' son by the Amazon Hyppolyta, and so is delighted to learn of Theseus' supposed death in battle. However when he returns, bringing a beautiful slave girl as a present for Hippolytus, Phaedra murders the girl. While Hippolytus is asleep she cannot resist kissing him but he awakes and repulses her. Furious at this rejection, she tells Theseus that he attempted to rape her; Theseus calls upon Poseidon to help avenge his honour and Poseidon arranges that Hippolytus falls from his horse while riding along the sea-shore and is killed. To the crowd around Hippolytus' body Phaedra confesses the truth and adds that she has taken poison. She dies still protesting her love.

17.   OEDIPUS, AND OTHER LEGENDS

The Delphic Oracle prophesied to King Laius of Thebes that he would have a son who would later kill his father and then marry his mother. Horrified by this prospect, Laius could see only one way to defeat the prophecy --- he stopped sleeping with his wife Jocasta; however she wasn't too pleased about this and one evening got him drunk, seduced him, and in due course gave birth to a son. Laius now had to tell Jocasta of the Oracle's prophecy; understanding now, she gave the baby to a shepherd with instructions that he be left on an exposed mountain to die, and as an extra precaution first pierced and then tied together the baby's feet. The shepherd however gave the baby to a man who took him home to Corinth, where he was adopted by the childless King Polybus and his wife Periboea. They gave him the name Oedipus, meaning "swollen feet", and brought him up as their son without telling him that he was adopted.

When he grew up Oedipus heard rumours that he was not the son of Polybus and Periboea, and went to Thebes to consult the Oracle there and learn the truth. However the Oracle, instead of answering his question, prophesied that he would kill his father and marry his mother. In Oedipus' mind this clearly referred to Polybus and Periboea and, determined to avoid any possibility of such horror, he decided not to return to Corinth. Soon, on a mountain pass in Thebes, he met an older man in a chariot with four servants; neither Oedipus nor the chariot party would give way to the other so the servants tried to force him aside; however Oedipus would not cede passage and was angrily prodded by the older man. Reacting furiously, Oedipus attacked and killed four of the group, only one servant escaping to the city to tell of the killing of King Laius, for it was of course he in the chariot. The first part of the Oracle's prophecy had been fulfilled.

Oedipus journeyed on to Thebes. The death of the king had not been properly investigated, for the city was at that time under siege by the terrible Sphinx, a creature with a winged-lion's body, and the face and breasts of a woman. Oedipus dealt with the Sphinx by correctly answering its riddle, and was consequently regarded as the saviour of the city. As a Prince of Corinth, he was invited to become Thebes' new king and additionally to take the widowed Queen Jocasta as his wife; he accepted these two offers and thus unknowingly completed the Oracle's prophecy. Jocasta in due course gave Oedipus two sons and two daughters.

Years later Thebes suffered from a plague and Oedipus sent Jocasta's brother Creon to the Oracle for advice. The plague, he was told, would clear when the killer of King Laius was punished. Oedipus called on the renowned blind seer Tiresias for help in locating Laius' killer but he, knowing the truth, refused to reveal it. Angered by this refusal, Oedipus accused Tiresias of plotting with Creon to seize the crown, whereupon Tiresias replied that "The killer of the king is a king and is in Thebes". This of course could have only one meaning, but Oedipus simply believed that Tiresias had gone mad; even Jocasta supported this view by relating the original prophecy and telling of the death of King Laius on a mountain road many years ago as showing that the Oracle could not always be believed. Oedipus vaguely remembered a similar event and asked her how many were there; many, she said, and all but one were killed. Beginning to suspect the awful truth, Oedipus immediately sent for the survivor, and told Jocasta what he remembered of the event all those years ago. She was relieved to hear this story, for she was able to point out that her baby son was left to die on the mountain, that his feet had been pierced and tied together to ensure he could not move, and that anyway according to the survivor her husband had been killed by a band of thieves. Oedipus however was disturbed by this for he remembered having problems with his feet as a youth.

A messenger arrived from Corinth with news of the death of King Polybus and Oedipus immediately felt a little better, for since he genuinely believed himself to be Polybus' son and of course had had no hand in his death, it was now clear that the Oracle's prophecy was wrong. But the messenger also disclosed that he was the man who had received the baby from the shepherd all those years ago and could thus tell Oedipus that he was actually the adopted son, not the natural son of Polybus. Jocasta immediately realised the truth behind these disclosures, begged Oedipus not to probe any further and went off to think about the consequences of what she had heard. He however still did not fully understand, and was determined to know the truth. Now the shepherd arrived; he and the messenger recognised each other and under Oedipus' relentless questioning, the full truth was disclosed, even to the detail that it was Jocasta herself who gave the baby to the shepherd. This final disclosure sent Oedipus rushing to the palace for Jocasta, only to find her dead; she had hanged herself, unable to face the reality of what had happened. In a fit of extreme agony over what he had now learned about himself, Oedipus tore from his mother's breast a golden brooch and blinded himself with its pin.

Stravinsky wrote **Oedipus Rex** entirely based on this legend, introducing only a Narrator who opens the opera by telling the audience that Oedipus' life was baited with a trap at the time of his birth.

Antigone

In the second play of Sophocles' trilogy the blind Oedipus, led by his daughter Antigone, went to Colonus, near Athens. King Theseus was the ruler there, who befriended Oedipus. Oedipus' two sons Etiocles and Polyneices were at war with each other over the succession to his throne, with Etiocles being supported by Jocasta's brother Creon. Oedipus' other daughter Ismene brought a message from the Oracle that whichever brother had the support of their father would win, and Creon also arrived to ask for Oedipus' support for Etiocles. Oedipus rejected Creon and cursed his two sons; Creon seized both Ismene and Antigone, intending also to take Oedipus, but Theseus intervened and saved them all. A roll of thunder announced to Oedipus that his death was near and he led his daughters and Theseus to the place near where he would die. He allowed only Theseus to go with him to that place.

In the third play of the cycle, Etiocles and Polyneices are both dead, having managed to kill each other, and Creon rules Thebes. He refused a burial for Polyneices and also forbade Antigone to return there to bury her brother. Antigone defied him and returned. Creon seized her and, even though she was his niece, ordered that she be buried alive. However his son Haemon, who was Antigone's lover, protested and told his father that his action was wrong. Tiresias, the blind seer who had previously so clearly intimated to Oedipus the truth about his life, also warned Creon that he must change his mind about Antigone or face the consequences. Convinced, Creon hurried back to countermand his order but was too late; Antigone had followed her mother Jocasta's example and hanged herself, and Haemon had also taken his own life. On returning to his palace, Creon then found that his wife Eurydice, having learned of Haemon's death, had also committed suicide.

None of the few operas on the *Antigone* play is in the repertoire.

Tiresias

He was the very long-lived blind prophet/seer from Thebes who is possibly best known for his part in Sophocles' *Oedipus* Trilogy. One version of how he came to lose his sight is that he happened upon Athena as she undressed and bathed; when she realised that she was being spied upon she was so furious that she immediately deprived him of his sight. Quickly regretting her angry reaction but unable to restore his sight, she compensated by giving him the gift of foresight.

An alternative version has Tiresias as the only person who, according to the legends, had ever lived both as a man and as a woman in the same lifetime. It is said that he saw a pair of snakes coupling, that he picked up and killed the female and that for this act was instantly transformed into a woman; some years later she came across another pair of mating snakes, and this time killed the male. This caused her to be restored to manhood. This experience made Tiresias the ideal person to be asked by Zeus and his wife Hera to resolve an argument they were having: did men or women enjoy sex more? To Hera's intense irritation he contradicted her view by answering that, on a scale of ten, women experienced pleasure at the ninth level compared to the man's pleasure at level one. She was so angered by this answer that she immediately deprived him of his sight. Zeus however provided some compensation by giving him the gift of deep insight and prophecy, together with a very long life.

"Les Mamelles de Tirésias" (*The Breasts of Tiresias*)   Poulenc, 1947

This is a fantasy comic-opera in which Thérèse becomes a man.

Act 1 Before the curtain goes up the Theatre Director appears and announces that it is time for everyone to make babies. When the curtain rises Thérèse is fed up with being a woman, and fed up with her husband. Deciding to change sex, she opens her clothes, releases her breasts (two balloons) which she bursts, and starts to grow a beard. Her husband initially thinks that the stranger wearing his wife's clothes must have murdered her, however she informs him that she is indeed his wife but is now a man and will in future be known as Tiresias; they go off together.

Act 2 Thérèse/Tiresias' husband has responded to the early exhortation to make babies by having over 40,000 in one day. Of course people want to know how this was done, but no explanation is offered. The Police Chief arrests Thérese/Tiresias, who chokes him; he revives, the husband tries to turn his wife back into a woman again by giving him/her new breasts (another pair of balloons) but he/she simply releases them into the air. The whole ludicrous comedy ends with a repeat of the call to make babies.

Alcestis

Alcestis, daughter of King Peleas of Iolcos, was the wife of King Admetus of Thessaly. When he became very ill and was close to death, his people prayed to the gods for his recovery. Their prayers were answered; Admetus could live, but only if someone else volunteered to die in his place. In spite of their deep affection for their king, none of his people loved him sufficiently to want to die for him; even his elderly parents weren't prepared to do that. But Alcestis, for love of her husband, offered herself as the replacement. Admetus immediately began to recover, and although delighted to be well again was horrified when he heard the price that had been paid for his life and went with his friend the great hero Hercules to the very gates of Hades to try and get his wife back. Hercules' presence there forced the gods to return Alcestis. Gluck's 1767 opera *Alceste* tells this story; it contains the very well-known aria *Divinités du Styx.*

PART 3. NORSE LEGENDS & "THE RING"

18.   THE RING

Like the Greeks (and Romans), the Scandinavians too had their mythological pantheon of gods and heroes; these are neither so extensive nor so interesting as the Greek ones and consequently there has been very little transfer of their stories into opera.   However Wagner, in his colossal *Ring* cycle, brought in many of the ideas and characters from these stories.   The principal elements he borrowed from the Nordic legends are:

Odin (also known as Woden, Wodan, Wotan) He was the chief god, who lived in a huge hall, called Valhalla.   He had 3 wives (Iord, Frigg,and Ring); two wolves; two ravens, which acted as his messengers and sources of information on everything that went on every-where; among his other possessions were a great spear, which was the symbol of his power, and a gold ring which had been forged by two dwarfs. He liked to wander around the world disguised as an old, grey-bearded, one-eyed man carrying a staff and wearing a wide-brimmed hat.

Valhalla The home of the gods.   This was a truly enormous place, so big that it had 540 doors, each wide enough to allow 800 people to pass through it abreast; the roof consisted of brightly polished shields supported by huge spears. Aside from the gods, the hall was intended for the use of heroes who had been killed in battle.   These were specially selected for Odin by a group of young women, the Valkyries, whose principal duty was to collect these dead heroes from the battlefield and take them to Valhalla.   There, the warriors would be revived, and then spend their days feasting, revelling and fighting. Odin needed these heroes as his future army against the time when it would be necessary to fight the race of Giants who lived in Jötunheim (Giantland).

Valkyries Warrior maidens, sometimes known as "the choosers of the slain", who were often regarded as the harbingers of war. They rode across the skies to the battlefields wearing shining helmets and breastplates, and carrying shields and flaming spears. The flickering lights of the "Aurora Borealis" were thought to be the reflections from their armour and spears. They sometimes had the power to influence the outcome of individual fights, and were responsible to Odin for making the selection of heroes to bring to Valhalla.

Brunhild A valkyrie. She had offended Odin and was sentenced to continuous sleep behind a ring of fire until she was rescued by a hero brave enough to pass through the fire to reach her. Such a man was Sigurd, who awoke her. They became engaged, but he still had a lot of adventuring to do so left her for a while, protected by the fire. At the Burgundian court he met Gunnar, with whom in due course he swore blood brotherhood. Sigurd was given a magic potion which caused him to forget Brunhild and fall in love with Gunnar's sister Gudrun, whom he married. He agreed to help Gunnar woo Brunhild and, disguised as Gunnar, leapt over the flames and brought her out. Learning later how she had been deceived, Brunhild arranged the murder of Sigurd but then, hearing that he was dead, she killed herself, leaving instructions that her body was to be burnt on the same funeral pyre as Sigurd's.

Norns The three fates who were constantly spinning the threads of human lives; they could cut or snap any of these threads at any time.

Ragnarök The time when, after years of weakening of moral fibre, the whole world is at war with itself. The Heavens break up; the gods rally to fight the Giants; Odin is killed; Thor, the most important of the gods after Odin, kills the Serpent of the World (a huge dragon) but himself dies poisoned by the dragon's breath. This is *Ragnarök*, the Doom of the Gods.

Wagner's other principal source for the *Ring* was a German epic poem, written around 1200AD, called *Nibelungenlied,* ("The song of the Nibelungs"). The Nibelungs are a race of dwarfs who live under the Rhine. The poem is clearly derived from the Norse legends.

In the first part we meet Kriemhild, a princess of Worms, in Burgundy, and Siegfried, a prince of the Lower Rhine. He arrives at Worms intent on marrying Kriemhild and is recognised by Hagen, an associate of Kriemhild's brother, King Gunther; he identifies Siegfried as a redoubtable hero who has acquired the Nibelung treasure; Siegfried owns a cloak that renders him invisible when he wears it; and his skin has the texture of horn, the result of bathing in dragon's blood, thus making him invincible in battle. Since King Gunther has to fight a war, Siegfried offers to lead the army, and on his victorious return is able to develop his courtship of Kriemhild.

There is news of a Queen Brunhild, a woman of outstanding beauty and strength, who will only marry a man who can match her. Gunther immediately knows that he wants this woman but would not be capable of winning her himself, so he enlists Siegfried's help, promising Siegfried his sister Kriemhild as a success prize. Together they go to Brunhild, with Siegfried disguised as Gunther's servant; Gunther beats Brunhild in all the contests since he merely goes through the motions, while Siegfried actually does all the work under his cloak of invisibility. Defeated, Brunhild accepts Gunther as her husband, and Siegfried gets Kriemhild as his bride. However, living in the same court as Gunther and Siegfried, Brunhild becomes suspicious about what may have happened; in a quarrel with Kriemhild she sneers at her for marrying a mere servant. Her suspicions are confirmed when Kriemhild tells her the real Gunther/Siegfried situation, even showing the ring and girdle Siegfried gave her which he had taken from Brunhild.

Brunhild is furious at the deception and plots with Hagen to get her revenge; now she befriends Kriemhild and, gaining her confidence, learns that Siegfried has a weak spot. She tells Hagen, who is able to kill him. Kriemhild, not surprisingly now starts to keep her distance from her brother Gunther and his man Hagen; she also arranges to bring Siegfried's treasure to the court, and starts to distribute it. This alarms Hagen as he fears for the greater influence this will bring her, so he siezes the treasure and sinks it in the Rhine

Attila, king of the Huns, arrives at the Court and asks to marry Kriemhild; she accepts him, seeing the possibility of an opportunity for revenge against Hagen some time in the future, and leaves Gunther's court to live with Attila. Some years later she persuades Attila to invite Gunther and Hagen, with retinue, to their palace; Hagen is wary of this invitation but can see no reason to turn it down. Once arrived, Kriemhild launches her attack; in the general fighting she has her brother killed and Hagen tied up. Hagen however refuses to tell her where he has concealed

Siegfried's treasure, so Kriemhild kills him herself, with Siegfried's sword. In turn, she is killed by one of her own knights, Hildebrand, who is appalled at her actions.

"Der Ring Des Nibelungen"   Wagner, 1876

The story is told in a cycle of four operas comprising a prologue and a trilogy, each part complete in itself, each carrying the story forward from the previous one. The 1876 date refers to the first complete performance of the entire cycle, which took Wagner 28 years to write.

Prologue: Das Rheingold (The Rhine Gold).

Scene 1: at the bottom of the river Rhine, where three Rhinemaidens guard the Rhine gold. Alberich, a Nibelung dwarf, tries to join them but they mock and tease him. However one of them tells Alberich that whoever could make a ring from this gold would become all-powerful, albeit at the cost of having to give up love. Alberich immediately forswears love, seizes an opportunity to steal the gold, and disappears.

Scene 2: within the battlements of Valhalla. Wotan, the principal god, is day-dreaming of his power and of the magnificent building he now inhabits, which was constructed for him by the giants Fasolt and Fafner. His wife Fricka reminds him of its price: unable to pay for it in any other way, Wotan promised the giants that they can have Freia, the goddess of youth, who is Fricka's sister. But the other gods are very unhappy about Wotan's deal; they need to protect Freia, for she is the one who grows the golden apples that enable them to keep their youth; however the giants remind them: it is Wotan's contract. Loge, the god of fire, arrives with a possible way out of the problem. He's heard of Alberich's theft of the gold, and of the ring forged from it; he and Wotan resolve to steal the gold and the ring, and give the gold to the giants as payment.

Scene 3: in a deep cave. Alberich's brother Mime has made a magic helmet which allows its wearer to assume any form he wishes. Alberich takes it and puts it on; he becomes invisible, then torments Mime by whipping him. He removes the helmet, organises a team of Nibelungs to carry off the gold, and then spots Wotan and Loge. He demonstrates his new powers by scaring off the Nibelungs and by turning himself into a giant snake. Loge suggests to Alberich that a small creature could probably more easily escape danger, but no doubt this would be too difficult for Alberich to manage. Not at all, says the snake, becoming a toad. Loge and Wotan capture him and carry him off with the gold.

Scene 4: up in the mountains. Alberich has had to give up the gold, and loses the ring too when Wotan forcibly takes it from him. Alberich then curses the ring: whoever has it will die. The giants enter with Freia, and demand that, to release her from the contract in exchange for gold, there must be sufficient of it to be piled up around her until she is completely covered. But even with all the gold now in the pile, including the helmet, there is still a chink of light and the giants demand the ring too, to fill the crack. Wotan refuses but Erda, the earth-goddess, appears and warns of the end of the gods, telling Wotan he must give up the ring. He concedes, and Freia is released, but immediately Alberich's curse on the ring starts working as Fasolt and Fafner begin to fight over it, leading to the death of Fasolt. Fafner takes the gold, the ring, and the helmet.

First Day: Die Walküre (The Valkyrie)

Wotan has provided Valhalla with protection in the form of nine daughters, the Valkyries, warrior women whose additional task is to bring the bodies of dead heroes, those killed in battle, to Valhalla where they are revived, and will help in its defence. The Valkyrie of the title is Wotan's favourite, Brünnhilde, a daughter of Erda (who is both goddess and earth mother). Siegmund and Sieglinde are twin brother and sister who were separated at an early age; human children of Wotan's by a mortal woman, they are part of Wotan's grand design to restore order by getting Siegmund to kill Fafner and return the ring to the Rhinemaidens.

Act 1 inside a house in the forest; there is a big tree within the house. A man staggers in, hoping for shelter from the storm outside. Hunding, the master of the house, is not in, but his wife gives the man water. Hunding returns and agrees that the man can stay the night. The stranger explains that he calls himself Wehwalt (Woeful) because he had returned with his father from the hunt one day to find his mother murdered and his twin sister gone; he no longer knew where his father was, and his life had been dogged by bad luck from that time. Worse still, having been asked for help by a woman who said she was being forced into marriage with someone she didn't love, he'd killed her brothers and was now on the run. Hunding reveals that he is one of her kinsmen; only the laws of hospitality prevent him from fighting the stranger there and then, but he tells "Woeful" that they will fight in the morning. Hunding and his wife go to their bedroom, and the stranger recalls his father's promise to provide him with a sword when he most needs it.

Hunding's wife returns. She has doped her husband's bed-time drink and shows the stranger a sword that had been thrust into the tree; it was put there by a one-eyed man when she married Hunding, and no-one has ever been able to pull it out. From a few gestures, expressions and words she realises that the stranger is her twin brother, Siegmund, and tells him that she is Sieglinde. He pulls the sword from the tree, they embrace and rush off.

Act 2 in Valhalla Wotan is aware of all that has been happening and that Hunding will soon catch up with the runaways. Brünnhilde is instructed that she must arrange for Siegmund to be the victor in the inevitable fight. She warns him however that he will have a fight on his own hands from his wife Fricka, for she is the goddess of marriage and is now approaching. Fricka insists that Hunding must win, to uphold the sanctity of marriage; that the incest of Sieglinde and Siegmund is an affront to nature; and that anyway Wotan's longer-term plans for Siegmund simply will not work. Wotan is eventually, reluctantly, persuaded by Fricka's arguments and tells Brünnhilde that she must not let Siegmund beat Hunding. It is Siegmund who must die. Brünnhilde protests, but her father threatens her with severest punishment if she disobeys him.

Scene 2. The fugitives enter; Sieglinde faints in Siegmund's arms. Brünnhilde appears and tells Siegmund that he will die and will go with her to Valhalla; he replies with great passion that he will not go without his sister and their soon-to-be-born child and that if necessary he will kill them first so that they can go with him. Brünnhilde finds this too much for her and decides to defy her father and protect Siegmund, knowing that this is what Wotan really wants anyway. Hunding arrives, battle is joined and Brünnhilde uses her shield to protect Siegmund from Hunding's spear; Wotan however intervenes, shatters Siegfried's sword against his spear, causing Brünnhilde to withdraw her shield in fear and thus allow Hunding's spear to kill Siegfried. "Go and tell Fricka she has been obeyed" Wotan instructs Hunding, with a gesture and look of such contempt that he drops dead. Brünnhilde picks up Sieglinde and the sword fragments, and rides off with her, pursued by a furious Wotan.

Act 3 is on the mountain. The Valkyries are there, each with a dead hero, intended for Valhalla, across her horse. The great chorus they sing at this gathering, popularly known as "The Ride of the Valkyries", is often played, without the chorus, as a concert piece. They are amazed to see Brünnhilde arrive with a woman, and a live one at that. However they are too afraid of Wotan to take their sister's part; Brünnhilde tells Sieglinde to go to the forest, where she will give birth to Siegfried, who will be the noblest hero in the world; then she faces Wotan's wrath. He tells her that her punishment is that she will no longer be a Valkyrie, and that she will lie in a deep magic sleep, unprotected, and vulnerable to the first man who finds her. She protests to her father, trying to justify her action in doing what she knew he really wanted, and succeeds in getting him to soften the sentence: her sleep will be protected by a wall of fire which will only be penetrable by a completely free, fearless hero. Loge is summoned to create the fire, and the sentence is implemented.

Second Day: Siegfried

Act 1 is by a cave in the forest. Mime is there, angry because he can achieve neither of the two tasks he has set himself. He cannot repair the broken sword he has, nor can he make a sword strong enough for Siegfried to be able to kill Fafner and regain the ring. Siegfried enters and confronts Mime, in whose cave he has always lived but whom he is beginning to detest, demanding some truths; Mime is not his real father, so who is? Mime tells him that a woman came from the forest and gave birth to a baby boy; she told Mime the boy was to be called Siegfried, gave him the broken pieces of the sword which had been shattered when the child's father was killed, and then she died. Siegfried is delighted with this story and, leaving the cave, tells Mime he *must* repair the sword.

A stranger enters; he wears a wide-brimmed hat, a cloak, and carries a spear as a staff. It is Wotan, in his Wanderer disguise. He persuades the reluctant Mime to ask him three questions, on which he, the Wanderer will stake his own life. Having answered them correctly, the situation is reversed but Mime can't answer the third question: who can weld the broken sword? Only a person who knows no fear! The Wanderer spares Mime's life, placing it in the hands of this unknown, and leaving Mime fearful. Siegfried returns and, impatient at Mime's failure to repair the sword, starts to re-forge it himself, refusing Mime's help. Now sensing something of Siegfried's destiny, and realising that it is from him that his life is at risk, Mime conceives the plan to take Siegfried to Fafner's lair to kill Fafner (who has turned himself into a dragon for greater protection) and learn fear in the process, thus becoming harmless to Mime; this would allow Mime to gain possession of the gold, and he would then secure his situation by poisoning Siegfried. Finishing the re-forging of the sword, Siegfried tests it by cutting the anvil in half; Mime crumbles in fright.

Act 2 in the forest outside Fafner's cave. The Wanderer approaches and confronts Alberich, who knows him to be Wotan. Alberich admits his inability to regain the gold, and is surprised when the Wanderer not only tells him of his brother Mime's plan to get it, but suggests waking the dragon to warn him; Fafner (the dragon) might then even give Alberich the ring to save himself. They do this but the dragon doesn't seem too interested. Siegfried is heard approaching; as the sound of his silver horn grows louder the dragon stirs and rears up to crush the intruder; Siegfried plunges his sword into the dragon's heart. As he dies, Fafner reveals Mime's plans to Siegfried. Some of his dragon's blood spills onto Siegfried's hand and, licking it off he finds he suddenly understands the song of one of the birds, telling him that *he* now owns Fafner's gold. Mime and Alberich appear, quarrelling about which one of *them* now owns the gold. As Siegfried emerges, carrying both the helmet and the ring, Mime offers him the poisoned drink but thanks to the dragon's blood Siegfried now understands Mime's real purpose and kills him with the sword. Feeling very alone now that he has killed Mime, he asks the bird for help in finding a companion and is told the story about Brünnhilde. Follow me, sings the bird, and I'll show you the way.

Act 3 at the foot of a mountain. The Wanderer rouses Erda from a sound sleep. Only half awake, she cannot deal with his questioning; confused, she is unclear even about who the Wanderer is and tells of being overpowered by Wotan and bearing Brünnhilde as a consequence. He forecasts the impending fall of the gods. Siegfried arrives, and finds the Wanderer barring his way; they threaten each other with spear and sword, the Wanderer telling Siegfried that his spear has already once broken the sword and will do it again. Triumphantly, Siegfried breaks the spear in two with his sword, compelling the Wanderer to withdraw. There is a rolling fire coming down the mountain and Siegfried plunges straight into it and at its top finds the sleeping Brünnhilde. Seeing her in armour he at first takes her for a man but, removing the armour and finding a female form, he experiences his first acute sensation of fear. He kneels down and kisses her. She awakes and they rapidly begin to appreciate each other. Suddenly she realises that previously she was a virginal Valkyrie, and not even a god had come near her; but now she is a woman, one who has already had some of her armour removed by a man, and she feels humiliated and afraid. Dismissing his own fears, Siegfried persuades her of their future together, and they embrace; nothing else matters any more, only their love is important.

The third day: Götterdämmerung (The twilight of the gods).

Prologue: On the rock where the Valkyries hang out, are three more of Erda's daughters, the Norns (the Fates).They are spinning the rope that holds the past, present and future together; the threads tangle, it breaks, and the sisters realise this is a sign of the end of the world.

Brünnhilde and Siegfried emerge, he in full armour and she leading her horse. He is off to perform more great deeds, and she gives him her horse, receiving the ring as a keepsake.

Act 1 King Gunther's Court. Alberich, from a loveless coupling with Gunther's mother, has an illegitimate son Hagen, who is scheming to regain the ring for his father. King Gunther, and his sister Gutrune, are therefore half-brother and sister to Hagen, who advises them that to secure their realm they should marry, and he suggests Brünnhilde and

Siegfried as their respective partners; he even suggests how these marriages can be effected. Gutrune will give Siegfried a magic drink that will cause him to forget about all other women and fall in love with the first woman he then sees, who of course will be Gutrune. Once she has won him for herself it will be easy for her to get him to win Brünnhilde for her brother Gunther. Siegfried's horn is heard, indicating his imminent arrival; he is invited into the Court and innocently accepts the doped drink, even dedicating it to Brünnhilde. With immediate effect he forgets her, becoming fascinated by Gutrune. Even when Gunther talks of a woman in an entranced sleep, protected by a ring of fire up on a mountain, a woman Gunther desires but cannot win, Siegfried fails to realise who it is, so powerful is the effect of the doped drink. But knowing that he has no fear of the fire, he offers to put on his magic helmet, disguise himself as Gunther, and try to win this woman for him. Siegfried and Gunther swear blood brotherhood and they set off for Brünnhilde's rock, leaving Hagen in charge at home.

Brünnhilde, outside her cave, listens to one of her sister Valkyries tell of Wotan's depression, just waiting for the foretold end of the gods. His only hope is that Brünnhilde should return the ring to the Rhinemaidens and thus break the curse. Brünnhilde refuses; to her it symbolises the love she bears for Siegfried. Siegfried's horn sounds his approach but to her surprise it is "Gunther" who appears, he fights with Brünnhilde, forcibly takes the ring from her finger, and takes her inside the cave.

Act 2 Back in Gunther's court, Alberich tells his son Hagen that they must press on with the plan for Siegfried's destruction and the recovery of the ring. Siegfried arrives, reports on the success of the plan to win Brünnhilde and says that Gunther is on his way back with her. When they arrive Brünnhilde is feeling pretty downcast at the turn of events but, suddenly seeing her ring on Siegfried's finger, furiously declares that *he* is her husband, accusing him of perjury. But he is still under the influence of the doped drink, and to clear himself swears an oath on Hagen's spear: let it kill him if he is lying about how he got the ring. Brünnhilde in turn swears revenge on Siegfried, and to achieve it tells Hagen that Siegfried can be defeated if he is struck in the back. By now almost everyone except Gutrune wants Siegfried's death (even Gunther has become suspicious about him), and they plan that it should be the result of a hunting "accident".

Act 3 in a forest by the Rhine. Siegfried has been briefly lured away from the hunt, and by the river bank talks to the Rhinemaidens who tell him he will die later that day if he keeps the ring, but he laughs at them and returns to the hunting party. Now Hagen slips another magic potion into his drink, this one the antidote to the first. Siegfried recalls for the company how he killed Fafner, how he came to understand the bird that led him to Brünnhilde, and of their passion after his awakening kiss. Wotan's two ravens fly over and Hagen asks Siegfried if he can understand them too. As Siegfried turns to look at them, Hagen plunges his spear into Siegfried's back.

At the court, where Siegfried's body has been taken, Hagen fights with and kills Gunther over the ring but when he reaches out to take it, Siegfried's dead hand rises up to prevent him. Brünnhilde, by now having realised something of the deception of which she was one of the victims, is appalled at what has happened; she has also come to understand about the curse of the ring and Wotan's wish to return it to the Rhinemaidens. She orders Siegfried's body to be placed on the funeral pyre; putting the ring on her finger, she lights the pyre, mounts her horse and rides into it; the fire will not only consume her body with Siegfried's but will also purify the ring for its return to the Rhinemaidens.

The Rhine overflows onto the flames, with the Rhinemaidens appearing on the waves, and Hagen rushes into the waters to try and recover the ring. Two of the Rhinemaidens drag him down into the water, while the third holds up the ring, recovered at last. As the hall of the court collapses, up in the sky is the sight of Valhalla, filled with its gods and heroes, gradually being consumed in its own fire and finally collapsing too. The only survivors of this double holocaust are Alberich and the Rhinemaidens, who between them had started the whole chain of events.

PART 4: SEX 'N' SEDUCTION

"The position is ridiculous, the pleasure momentary and the expense damnable."

The Earl of Chesterfield (attrib).

Aldous Huxley, in his "Heaven and Hell", quoted another view on this subject: "'Bed' as the Italian proverb succinctly puts it 'is the poor man's opera'", which maybe throws another light on the significance of sex in opera. Highly sexed men with a strong libido, e.g. Don Juan and Casanova types, litter the operatic stages: men with an easy charm for women, able to "bed" a woman with not much more than a meaningful glance (the Duke of Mantua in *Rigoletto* for instance). There are very few opera stories about the many "Doña Juanitas" who inhabit the same world as men and who are capable of far more effective seduction if only because men have less powers of resistance in these matters (perhaps that's why women's exploits are less celebrated; it's all too easy for them), and where they do occur in opera the lady is usually some legendary magician/goddess such as Circe in Homer's Odyssey. Carmen is one of the few "real" women playing such a role.

In life of course there are far more women who are irresistible to men than there are men to women, but given man's much weaker nature in this regard this need not be a matter for further comment. But sometimes in real life, when an irresistible male seducer actually appears who also happens to be a very talented writer, this second quality can stimulate him into producing some extremely good stories around the subject of seduction. Women, I suspect, regard such stories with amusement as just another male fantasy, and dismiss the real-life examples either as just further examples of typical male exploitation of their more simple-minded sisters, or simply regard the man as some kind of one-off freak. Whatever, there are enough real-life examples of practised male seducers for us to know that this may be an exotic but not a rare species. Don Juan and Casanova are two of the best known of these and, at least in the case of Don Juan, have become so as much by the quality of the writing about them as for their exploits; but also, and more particularly for him, by the quality of Mozart's music in his opera of this title.

19.   LIBERTINES & LOVERS

It is uncertain whether or not **Don Juan** was a real historical character; the case for or against is unproven. But if he were real he would most likely have been one Don Juan Tenorio de Sevilla, a 16th-century Spanish libertine whose exploits formed the basis of over 40 operas. But real or not, he is a very popular figure in literature as an expert seducer. A Spanish monk, Tirso, told the tale in 1630 of a Don Juan who, after three successful seductions, had his fourth narrowly fail due to the intervention of the girl's father. Don Juan killed the father in the duel which followed this intervention but then later, in the cemetery, came across the father's grave complete with a stone statue over it; the statue gripped Don Juan and hurled him into hell without even the opportunity of confession. A later variation on this has Don Juan mockingly inviting the statue to dinner and this idea entered into a number of the later *Don Juan* stories and operas; the whole genre culminated in Mozart's great work on the subject, *Don Giovanni*, after which it is doubtful if any later opera composer would care to submit himself to direct comparison with such a sublime creation.

More real than Don Juan, but equally a character with a sharp eye and a taste for a pretty woman, was the notorious **Casanova**, who certainly did exist. Giovanni Giacomo Casanova, Chevalier de Seingalt (1725-1798), was a Venetian who, as a young man, took holy orders and a position in a seminary; he was however expelled over a scandal. He travelled in Italy and Europe before returning to Venice, where he lived on a combination of his great charm and considerable gambling skills. He was arrested for his activities in dabbling in the occult and sentenced to five years' imprisonment in one of Venice's most fearsome prisons, but made a sensational escape. He went to Paris and there established and directed the French Lottery, whilst enjoying the favours of innumerable women, a great many of whom were celebrated in his 12 volumes of *Memoirs*. Much of what is known about Casanova, particularly concerning his very many liaisons with women, derives from these Memoirs, so this may be a case of a man writing his own reputation for posterity. He resumed his travels, but was expelled from Vienna, and then had to flee from Paris to escape his creditors. He returned to Venice, now as a spy for the State, but again was forced to leave. He eventually "semi-retired" to Germany, where he found work as a secretary and librarian, and wrote his *Memoirs*, which became the source for a number of operas based on his life.

His acquaintance was claimed by the librettist Lorenzo da Ponte, who was no mean "Casanova" type himself and who collaborated with Mozart in three operas; his clever and witty libretto for *Don Giovanni* adds hugely to the work's great popularity. The "Don Juan" and "Casanova" stories are examples of a theme that seemed to draw the best from men with a similarly easy success rate with women, such as da Ponte himself (at least to judge by *his* own 'Memoirs').

Lorenzo da Ponte was, for the first years of his life, Emanuele Conegliano, the eldest of three sons of Jewish parents. Their father, at the age of forty and widowed, wished to re-marry (he had a 16-year-old Catholic girl in mind) and decided that he and his sons should become

Christians in order to facilitate this desirable end. The local Bishop, one Lorenzo da Ponte, converted the family and in the custom of the time the converts adopted the surname of their Sponsor. Emanuele additionally chose for himself the first name of Lorenzo. When he grew up the "new" Lorenzo da Ponte also became a priest, then went to Venice and indulged in a passionate affair with a girl there; he became addicted to gambling and left the city for a teaching job in a seminary, from which he was soon expelled for seditious writings. He was offered financial support and accommodation by an older man but couldn't resist the opportunity of seducing the man's young mistress and so had to leave; later, at other lodgings he was again thrown out, this time for making love to his landlady's daughter-in-law. And all of this time he was, like the Bishop who converted him, an accredited priest in the Catholic faith. Thus the good Bishop, who would otherwise by now have been decently forgotten, has, through no fault of his own, had his name forever linked with a range of activities of which he would surely not have approved. But, if you go around converting God's Chosen People, perhaps one may expect God to get His own back from time to time!

Lorenzo the convert met and became friends with Casanova (or so he claimed in his *Memoirs*, written when he was in his sixties and living in North America) and, so he claimed again there, wrote the libretti for *Don Giovanni* and two other operas simultaneously in nine weeks, having only the comfort and stimulation of a box of snuff, plenty of wine, and his then landlady's daughter. In his time da Ponte was a priest, poet and writer in Italy, a bookseller in London, a fugitive from justice, a greengrocer, a wine-merchant, and a professor of Italian at Columbia University. He was influential in New York in arranging for the première there of *Don Giovanni,* which was given by the extraordinarily talented Garcia family, then comprising Manuel Garcia (composer, tenor, and singing teacher), his wife Joaquina (soprano), his son Manuel (baritone, who would later establish a huge reputation as the greatest teacher of singing of his time), and elder daughter Maria who was to become the world-famous mezzo-soprano Maria Malibran. The Garcia family talent was, a few years later, rounded off by the development of the younger daughter who, as Pauline Viardot, would achieve a world-wide fame, also as a mezzo, that came to equal that of her sister Maria.

Mozart completed the composition of *Don Giovanni* in Prague, at a villa owned by a retired lady who had a generous and open-hearted lifestyle, probably developed during her earlier simultaneous careers as both an opera singer and as mistress to a wealthy nobleman. The latter's contributions to her lifestyle quite possibly went a good way towards the purchase of the villa, which she acquired when eventually she left him and the opera scene, married her former teacher and settled down to live the good life by providing a warm and welcoming centre for the musicians, actors and writers of Prague. It was during rehearsals for the first performance of his new work, given in Prague, that Mozart, supposedly not happy with the sound of Zerlina's scream when the Don makes his moves upon her, and unable to get her to scream convincingly, made his own moves by concealing himself behind her and giving her an (in)appropriate pinch at the appropriate moment. "That's the sound I want" he told her, as she then really screamed. Zerlina, played by the wife of the theatre manager, was presumably then able to reproduce this sound without further encouragement.

"Don Giovanni" Mozart, 1787

The Rake punished, or Don Giovanni to give the work its full title, opens with Leporello, the Don's manservant, complaining about always having to wait outside while his master is inside enjoying himself; suddenly the Don rushes out in a bid to escape an enraged Donna Anna. Her father, the Commendatore, follows her but Don Giovanni kills him in a duel. Returning with her fiancé Don Ottavio, only to find her father dead, Donna Anna swears revenge. Donna Elvira appears; in her aria she tells of having been tricked into a false marriage and then abandoned by Don Giovanni, but Leporello tells her his master's like that, she's not the only girl to have been fooled, and in the "Catalogue" aria he tells her of the numbers of girls in different countries that the Don has had, so many that he doesn't even bother to add up the totals he gives, but 2065 in all. (Possibly this catalogue aria was drawn from da Ponte's own personal experience!) The effect is to induce in Elvira a desire to avenge herself.

Don Giovanni's attentions are now focused on the newly engaged Zerlina, a country girl from near his estate. He instructs Leporello to take the villagers, including Zerlina's fiancé, on a tour of the estate whilst he makes headway with the girl; however his progress is interrupted first by the appearance of Elvira, who tells Zerlina a thing or two about the man she's attracted to, and then by the arrival of Donna Anna and her fiancé requesting his help in locating her father's murderer. He leads Elvira off-stage to ease the situation and whilst he's distracted in this way Anna realises he is the man she'd had to fight off in her bedroom when her subsequent flight led directly to the death of her father.

Zerlina meanwhile has to explain to her fiancé that, after all, nothing actually *happened*, and they later attend a party in the Don's castle. He immediately resumes his attack on Zerlina's virtue and a little later the party is interrupted by a scream from her. She is off-stage in a locked room with Don Giovanni, but before the party-goers can break down the door he opens it and appears apparently marching Leporello before him at sword-point; in the general confusion they both escape through the garden windows.

The next act opens with Leporello telling his master that he wishes to leave his service and with Don Giovanni having to retain him with a handsome bribe; OK says Leporello, but you've got to give up women. "What! They're more necessary to me than breath and bread!" And anyway since it's all done for love of women it would be cruel to all the others if I tried to be faithful to just one. And anyway Leporello, I need your help with my plans for Donna Elvira's pretty little maid. They swap hats and cloaks and Elvira is induced to go off with, as she thinks, Don Giovanni, whilst he is now able to prepare for his move on the maid. However he is interrupted and has to make a hurried exit. He later meets up with Leporello in the churchyard where there happens to be a large statue of the late Commendatore. Leporello has had some unfortunate experiences due to being mistaken for his master, and Don Giovanni rubs salt into the wound by telling of his own good fortune in meeting a young girl who thought he was Leporello and was exceedingly affectionate towards him! Suddenly the moonlight breaks through and illuminates the statue; at the same time, a voice calls out "Your joking will end before dawn". Suspecting the statue, they read its inscription: "Here I wait for vengeance on the impious man who killed me". The Don decides that this is a joke that must have a follow-through and mocks his murdered victim by inviting the statue to dinner; the statue accepts the invitation.

The final scene is in Don Giovanni's banqueting hall, where he is enjoying a substantial dinner; it is interrupted by Donna Elvira, who still carries a torch for him; he plays with her feelings and then resumes his dinner. There is a second interruption; now it's the large stone statue of the Commendatore. Stating that one who has eaten heavenly food has no need of the earthly variety, the statue invites Don Giovanni to dine with him instead. Refusing to be over-awed the Don accepts, shakes the statue's hand and then is unable to release himself from its grip. In spite of urgings from the statue to repent, he refuses and orders it to leave, managing at last to free his hand. "Your time is up" the statue tells him, and the whole place goes up in flames as the voice announces Don Giovanni's eternal damnation.

Perhaps the most appropriate epitaph for Don Giovanni, or Casanova, or any other of their ilk, might be the description given of another real-life Casanova type, Lord Byron, by Lady Caroline Lamb, who was just one of the many ladies who succumbed to *his* fascinations: "...mad, bad, and dangerous to know".

Mozart, 1790

"Così fan tutte"

Another of da Ponte's librettos to focus on the business of seduction is Mozart's *Così fan tutte*, in which Ferrando and Guglielmo are praising the faithfulness and virtue of Dorabella and Fiordiligi, the two sisters to whom they are respectively engaged. Their friend Don Alfonso challenges their views and says that if they will co-operate with him, following implicitly all his directions, he will prove to them that the two girls are no different from the rest of their sex, for all women are fickle.

Readily accepting such an easy bet, Ferrando and Guglielmo agree to pretend that they have suddenly been called away to their army units to go to war; but then to re-appear disguised as Albanian officers who are to try and seduce the sisters. Only now each must seduce the other's fiancée. After their initial sortie, when both retire rebuffed, they congratulate each other on proving how right they were in their judgements of the sisters' virtue. But Don Alfonso is not finished yet and reminds them that they agreed to follow his orders for two whole days. He enlists the help of Despina, maid to Fiordiligi and Dorabella, who encourages them, whilst they have the opportunity of their fiancés being away, to have some fun with the two handsome Albanian officers. The sisters succumb to these persuasions and to the pleadings of the 'Albanians' and yield their hearts (but not their bodies, it's not that kind of a story), even agreeing to marry them.

Having made his point and won his bet, Don Alfonso unscrambles the plot, to the serious embarrassment of the now not quite so virtuous sisters, and everything seems to end happily; *seems,* because the text is unclear as to exactly what happens, which sister marries which officer. But after all, as Don Alfonso reminds them, he said at the outset: "Così fan tutte... all women are like that."

Figaro: was he Beaumarchais?

Da Ponte's third libretto for Mozart was also what has proved to be one of his finest, *The Marriage of Figaro*; he took his storyline from the play of the same name by Beaumarchais, who wrote a trilogy of plays about his Figaro character, the first two of which are recognised as *his* masterpieces. These were adapted for opera librettos, and now Rossini's *The Barber of Seville* and Mozart's *The Marriage of Figaro* are among the most popular operas in the world, part of every opera company's repertoire.

Beaumarchais

Pierre Auguste Caron de Beaumarchais was an adventurer. He was an arms dealer, a would-be slave dealer, an inventor, a man of advanced socio-political thinking, a highly popular writer and playwright, a secret agent for the King of France, and a contributor to the success of the American War of Independence. He had three prison sentences on his record and was only released from the last one by the personal efforts of one of his ex-mistresses. Needless to say he was also a great charmer of women, but a ruthless one to boot. Wanting to influence the outcome of a court case, he gave many gifts to a woman so that she might influence her husband's mind in the affair, but she was unsuccessful and the case was decided against Beaumarchais. The wife very properly returned all the gifts, keeping only one; Beaumarchais sued her for its return too. The counter-suit by the lady's husband resulted in a huge scandal and the first of Beaumarchais' prison sentences.

In his early years he was just Pierre Auguste Caron, the son of a watchmaker; he worked with his father and mastered the skills of his trade to such a degree that he was able to invent a clock movement which later became the subject of patent litigation (which he lost), and which then eventually led him into the gifts scandal and then to his first successful writing venture. His father dismissed him from his employment for reason of his conduct, the sort of conduct that so fascinated one of his father's customers, a wealthy widow, that she married him. Among her estates was a property called Beaumarchais, which allowed Pierre Auguste Caron to improve his own name significantly. His wife died not long after they married.

Beaumarchais' total lack of morals, combined with a tremendous self-confidence, so impressed a wealthy businessman that he engaged him as an intermediary, first for dealings in England, and then in Spain where Beaumarchais tried but failed to get a monopoly of the slave trade to the Spanish Colonies. Nevertheless these activities provided him with substantial wealth, enhanced by marriage to another wealthy widow who also died soon after the wedding. Following his unsuccessful court case, which cost him a lot of money, he wrote his *Mémoires* in which he presented his own side of that story in his own words; the book sold extremely well and not only established his reputation as a writer but also restored some of his wealth.

Soon after, he published *The Barber of Seville,* which was immensely successful. Louis XV became his patron and sent him abroad as a secret agent. It is said that Beaumarchais strongly influenced Louis' decision to support the American Colonists in their fight for independence and that he was personally responsible for recruiting volunteers and organising a fleet to take them to America for the fighting. He also lent the rebels large sums of money (which were only partially repaid by the American Government).

Beaumarchais then wrote *The Marriage of Figaro* as a sequel to *The Barber* but public performances were banned because of its improper attitudes towards the nobility; they were so irritated by the play that they managed to have Beaumarchais imprisoned over it and it was several years before a public performance was permitted. His third play, *La mère coupable*, although achieving a limited initial success, never acquired the popularity of the earlier two; it was not until 1966 that Milhaud created an opera from it, which had even less success than the play.

Then came the French Revolution; Beaumarchais lost a lot of money trying to import muskets to help the Revolutionaries, but this did not prevent them from declaring him an *émigré* and confiscating his property. He was again imprisoned, but later released and died in relative poverty.

Beaumarchais was a fixer, a schemer, something of a womaniser, a man of advanced social ideas for his time and background, a supporter of both the American Revolution and the French Revolutionary ideals of *Liberté, Egalité, Fraternité*; yet he was also a man who was capable of trying to make money out of one of the most anti-social of all human activities, the slave trade. This highly intelligent, witty and literate man might well, it has been speculated, have seen himself as a kind of model for two of his own literary characters: *Figaro*, as himself in his prime; and *Cherubino*, as himself in adolescence. Both possibilities seem to me to be very reasonable propositions.

If the distillation of a masterwork by Beaumarchais into a masterly adaptation by da Ponte then has Mozart's genius poured over it, the quality of the result is surely inevitable. But before looking at *The Marriage* it makes sense to look at *The Barber*, since this is where some of the principal characters first appear.

"The Barber of Seville" Rossini, 1816

The Barber was an extremely popular opera even before Rossini wrote a note, for it had already been set by Paisiello, whose work was so well liked that people took against Rossini for thinking he could produce something as good; the resultant antipathy gave Rossini's effort a hard time until it finally proved itself to be the better work, and his is the one that has survived.

In Seville Count Almaviva, in the guise of the poor student Lindoro, is courting Rosina, the ward of Dr. Bartolo, who intends to marry her himself. Almaviva meets and enlists the help of Figaro, who in a bravura and very witty aria 'Largo al Factotum' introduces himself as the barber and general factotum to all and sundry. Using a "cover" thought up by Figaro, Almaviva manages to get into Dr. Bartolo's house and tells Rosina that he is Lindoro, a poor student. Dr. Bartolo and Don Basilio, Rosina's music teacher, are both suspicious of "Lindoro" and try to get him out; they are also concerned to hear of the arrival of the wealthy Count Almaviva in the city.

Figaro now arranges for Almaviva to go back to the house, this time as Don Alonso, standing in for the "suddenly ill" Don Basilio; Dr. Bartolo accepts this story and leaves "Don Alonso" alone with Rosina for her music lesson while he goes off to have a shave from Figaro, who then manages to steal a key which will allow Almaviva and Rosina to escape that night. Don Basilio turns up, perfectly well, but a decent bribe from Almaviva shuts him up.

Bartolo however is becoming suspicious and, deciding to bring forward his marriage to Rosina, sends Don Basilio off to bring a notary. He then convinces Rosina that Lindoro clearly doesn't love her because he's found out that Lindoro is merely acting on behalf of this Count Almaviva. Lindoro returns and confesses to Rosina that he and the Count are the same person and they decide to act on their escape plan; but because the balcony ladder provided by Figaro has been removed, they can't. Don Basilio arrives with the notary and, with the encouragement of another bribe, this time from Figaro, performs the marriage of Rosina to Almaviva. Dr. Bartolo realises he's been outwitted, accepts the marriage and consoles himself with the thought that at least he doesn't have to find a dowry.

"The Marriage of Figaro"   Mozart, 1786

Figaro has now joined Count Almaviva as his valet/manservant and is preparing for his own marriage to Susanna, Countess (Rosina) Almaviva's maid. Susanna believes that their new room is too near that of the Count, for she is aware of his less than chaste feelings for her. Figaro had earlier made a promise to Marcellina, a duenna in the Count's household, to marry her if he was not able to repay a loan, and now she and Dr. Bartolo, the Countess's former guardian, are trying to stop his marriage to Susanna and to hold him to his agreement. The Count's young page Cherubino (christened Leon de Asturga, but universally known by his nickname "little cherub"), who is having huge problems coping with his hormones and is losing the battle, is telling Susanna of his hopeless passion for the Countess, when the Count arrives; Cherubino hides and is a witness to the Count's moves on Susanna. Don Basilio arrives and in turn the Count has to hide, forcing Cherubino into another hiding place. Don Basilio tells Susanna that everyone knows about the Count's feelings for her, and also tells her the gossip about Cherubino's love for the Countess.

The Count can't stand for this and comes out of hiding; he tells Susanna about Cherubino being found with Barberina, the gardener's daughter, and then discovers Cherubino. Deeply embarrassed by the realisation that Cherubino must have observed his attempt on Susanna, he dismisses the boy, ordering him to join the army.

Unhappy because she feels that the Count no longer loves her, the Countess, with the assistance of Susanna and Figaro, decides to set him up. Susanna will send him a letter inviting him to a clandestine meeting, but Cherubino will go instead in her clothes and the Countess will suddenly appear. In the Countess's room she and Susanna are fitting Cherubino with a suitable outfit when the Count knocks; Cherubino is hastily pushed into the dressing room and the door locked. The Countess explains that the noises were due to Susanna trying on her wedding dress, but the Count is not satisfied and goes off to get some tools to force open the dressing room; as he leaves he locks the main door to ensure that whoever may be in there can't get out. Cherubino quickly jumps out of the window and Susanna disappears into the dressing room. She reappears when the Count returns, and he is forced to apologise for his suspicions.

Figaro tries to escape Marcellina's determination to hold him to his earlier promise by explaining that he cannot marry without his parents' consent, and shows a birthmark on his arm as proof of his supposed noble descent; amazingly, Marcellina recognises this and knows him for her own long-lost son. Susanna enters in the middle of their embrace and is furious to find him in the arms of another woman, but everything is satisfactorily explained.

That night, in the garden, Figaro comes across Barberina who tells him she has a message from the Count to Susanna, causing him to think that Susanna is already deceiving him with the Count. The Countess and Susanna appear in each other's clothes, Cherubino flirts with the 'Countess' (actually Susanna), the Count flirts with 'Susanna' (actually his wife), and Figaro recognises Susanna by her voice. The Count at last understands that he's been tricked, apologises to his wife, receives her forgiveness, and everything ends happily.

In this opera Mozart was among the first to recognise the approaching end of the *castrati* phenomenon by writing Cherubino's part for a woman's voice, not a castrato's, but in this he also probably recognised Beaumarchais' own sense of the theatrical appeal of such an idea when he insisted for his own play, the original of the opera, "that Cherubino could be played only by a young and very pretty woman."

Beaumarchais' third play of his trilogy is *La mère coupable* ("The guilty mother"). The virtuous Countess, in a moment of madness, allows herself to be seduced by Cherubino, and bears an illegitimate child as a consequence. Later, Cherubino is killed off in a distant land.

"Chérubin" Massenet, 1905

In Mozart's *Marriage of Figaro* the Count fired Cherubino and ordered him to join the army. Chérubin here is now a young officer and, at his own 17th birthday party, is still having huge hormonal problems; he is simply overwhelmed by every beautiful woman he meets. A duel with an irate Count over a letter he sent to the Countess is averted by Nina, Count Almaviva's ward who secretly loves him; she persuades the Count that the letter was intended for herself but somehow went astray. At the party Chérubin enjoys an hour of love with the royal mistress, who is the guest of honour; he receives love tokens from the Baroness and the Countess; survives their fury when his hour of love becomes public knowledge; and finally runs off with Nina. "C'est Don Juan!" remarks one of the characters, appropriately.

"Le Comte Ory" Rossini, 1828

Count Ory was another real-life "Don Juan", whose activities were recorded first in a popular ballad of the 18th century and then again later, in the early 19th century in a short vaudeville play. Rossini then wrote him more deeply into the records with this witty and tuneful opera.

Act 1 The setting is the Castle of Formoutiers; it is around 1200 AD, and the men of the castle are away at the Crusade; the ladies there have sworn against having men in the castle during the absence of the Crusaders. Count Ory has established himself outside the walls, disguised as a hermit but with intentions on the honour of Adèle, sister of the absent Lord of the castle His disguise is so effective that even his own page, Isolier, doesn't recognise him, though he has suspicions. Notwithstanding these doubts, Isolier consults the "hermit" on his own plans concerning Adèle's virtue; he proposes to enter the castle disguised as a pilgrim. The "hermit" is both very impressed with this plan and concerned to learn that his own page has become a rival in his seduction strategy.

The ladies, hearing of the "hermit's" wisdom, leave their fortress to consult him; he takes the opportunity to advise Adèle to be wary of the "pilgrim" who, he informs her, is the page of the notorious Count Ory. His own disguise and duplicity are however exposed at the same time as it is announced that the Crusaders will return in a day's time. Disappointed but not downhearted, he reflects that there's still a day in hand to get what he wants.

Act 2 In the Castle the women are all angry over the deception. Outside there is a storm and pleas for shelter from a party of nuns. They are of course Count Ory's men, led by him as their "Mother Superior". Once inside, the "nuns" soon discover the wine cellar, but Ory is now recognised by his page Isolier who lays a trap for him. With Adèle's co-operation he arranges an assignation for Ory with Adèle; in the darkened bedroom Ory hears Adèle's voice but, moving on her, finds that he is actually wooing and embracing his own page Isolier. Trumpets announce the return of the Crusaders, and the Count and his men have to escape quickly. Adèle's virtue just about remains intact for, having developed quite a fancy for the page Isolier, who knows what might have developed if the Crusaders had been delayed.

Falstaff, Oldcastle and The Merry Wives of Windsor

Of literature's best known seducers the most famously unsuccessful must be Sir John Falstaff, Shakespeare's rascally comic drunkard, buffoon and wit whom he introduced in *King Henry IV Pt.1,* developed in *King Henry IV Pt.2* and disposed of (in death) in *King Henry V.* However Sir John's popularity was such, particularly with Queen Elizabeth who was reputed to have expressed a wish for a play about Falstaff in love, that Shakespeare wrote a further adventure, *The Merry Wives of Windsor,* giving Sir John the entertaining plan of trying to seduce two respectable married ladies. This play in turn became the basis for Verdi's final (and only comic) opera ***Falstaff.*** The falstaffian character had become so popular in the *Henry IV* plays, in which he was a crony of Prince Hal, the Prince of Wales, that in the epilogue to *King Henry IV Pt.2* Shakespeare wrote:

> *"If you be not too cloyed with fat meat, our humble author will continue the story, with Sir John in it, and make you merry with fair Katherine of France: where, for anything I know, Falstaff shall die of a sweat, unless already he be killed with your hard opinions; for Oldcastle died a martyr, and this is not the man".*

"Oldcastle" was Sir John Oldcastle, Shakespeare's original real-life model for the character of Falstaff and whose name he had intended to use. Sir John Oldcastle had been a soldier and somewhat discredited friend of Prince Hal, Prince of Wales and later King Henry V; he was also one of the leaders of the Lollards, the anti-clericalist movement established by John Wycliffe, but his Royal connections could not (or perhaps would not) save him from being arrested, thrown into the Tower and sentenced to death on charges of heresy for his advocacy of Lollard principles. He soon escaped and promptly joined a plot to kidnap his former friend, now the King; this failed, and Oldcastle went on the run, evading capture for three years before being brought to book and again incarcerated in the Tower. His previous sentence was still in force and this time there was no escape; he was executed in December 1417, by hanging and burning.

His descendants quickly objected to the use of their forebear's name being given to such a disreputable character as Shakespeare had drawn and were able to insist that the name was changed. "Falstaff" was chosen, perhaps to suggest a "false staff" for the Prince to depend on, yet Shakespeare still managed to get a subtle reference to his original model when Prince Hal, in *Henry IV Pt.1,* refers to Falstaff as "my old lad of the castle", and directly of course in the epilogue quoted above. Following his appearances in *Henry IV Pts.1&2,* then in *The Merry Wives,* he gets a "passing" reference in *Henry V* where his death is reported.

"Falstaff"   Verdi, 1893

Verdi's opera is set in Windsor in the reign of King Henry IV. At "The Garter Inn" Falstaff has been presented with the bill for a night of drinking with his old friends Bardolph and Pistol, and with Dr. Caius; however he cannot pay. He tells Bardolph and Pistol that the Mistresses Ford and Page (Shakespeare's *Merry Wives*), are both attracted to him, that he will seduce them both as a means of getting at their husbands' money, and in fact has already written a letter to each; he needs only to have the letters delivered, and assigns this small task to Messrs. Bardolph and Pistol. However even these old rogues refuse to have anything to do with such dishonesty, and for their pains receive a lecture from Falstaff on honesty and his philosophy of life.

Scene 2 is in the garden of Ford's house. Mistress Ford and Mistress Page have received their letters and are highly amused to discover that the letters are identical; they decide to play Falstaff at his own game. Master Ford enters with Fenton, a young man in love with Ford's daughter Nannetta, and with the elderly Dr. Caius who is also courting Nannetta, and also Bardolph and Pistol; these two tell him of Falstaff's plan to seduce his wife and get at his money. Mistresses Ford and Page enlist the help of Mistress Quickly, a neighbour and servant to Dr. Caius, to arrange an assignation with Falstaff; Master Ford determines to visit Falstaff to investigate this story of Bardolph and Pistol; and Fenton takes Nannetta to a secluded corner where they engage in a little kissing.

Act 2 Scene 1, is back at "The Garter Inn". Bardolph and Pistol re-ingratiate themselves with Sir John and introduce Mistress Quickly who has come to inform Falstaff that both ladies do indeed love him but that at the moment only Mistress Ford can see him and, conveniently, her husband is out every day between two and three. Falstaff is impressed. An Italian gentleman, Maestro Fontana, arrives, to tell Falstaff that he, Fontana, is in love with Mistress Ford, that he's tried unsuccessfully to seduce her and here is a bag of gold for Falstaff if he can achieve this desirable objective. To Falstaff, who doesn't see through Ford's disguise, this will be easy money since he'll be seeing the lady anyway, by her own invitation in a half-hour, and he goes off to dress for conquest.

Scene 2 is in a room in Ford's house. Mistress Quickly reports that Falstaff will be coming very soon; Nannetta is dismayed by her father's wish that she should marry Dr. Caius. Falstaff arrives, and everyone other than Mistress Ford hides. He tells her how beautiful she is, how handsome he once was, immediately proposes, and finds that he really is too fat to be able to embrace her. But Ford is on his way, and Falstaff has to hide behind a screen. Ford and his men search everywhere for Falstaff but overlook the screen. When they turn their attention to another room Falstaff is bundled into a dirty linen basket, and then tipped out via the window into the river below.

Act 3 Scene 1, is back at the Inn again. Falstaff is depressed over the outcome of what should have been a very straightforward bit of seduction, and helps himself to wine to cheer himself up. Mistress Quickly arrives to tell him that what happened wasn't Alice's fault for she still loves him, as the letter she's sent him via Mistress Quickly confirms; she wants to meet him at midnight, suitably disguised, in the Royal Park. The letter doesn't of course tell him that she and her husband are fully reconciled. As they go off, Ford and Dr. Caius appear, to plot the marriage of Dr. Caius, who will also be suitably disguised, to Nannetta that same night.

Scene 2 is in Windsor Park at midnight. Fenton and Nannetta meet to complete their own plot and go off; Falstaff arrives dressed as a huntsman and on the stroke of midnight Alice arrives. His clumsy attempts at lovemaking are interrupted by the arrival of a group of fairies, led by Nannetta as their Queen; Falstaff, who believes it is unlucky to look on fairies, hides behind a tree. In due course everyone comes on stage in appropriate disguise and sets about their common target, Sir John Falstaff, until he can stand no more and is finally forgiven. Ford goes ahead with the marriage of his daughter to Dr. Caius only to find, too late, that the "bride" was Bardolph, who took over the role of Queen of the fairies; Ford also discovers that he's been totally outwitted by his daughter when he learns that the other marriage he approved was that of Nannetta to Fenton, also in disguise.

The German composer Otto Nicolai also used Shakespeare's play for his 1849 opera *Die lustigen Weiber von Windsor* ("The Merry Wives of Windsor"), but this opera, though popular in Germany, is only known elsewhere for its very attractive overture.

"Der Rosenkavalier" *(The Knight of the Rose)* **Richard Strauss, 1911**

This is a whole opera about sex. The opening scene, which is set in the bedroom of the Princess Werdenberg, follows a brief overture of which it has been said that, from its climax, we know exactly what went on before the curtain rose. With her husband away, the Princess has just spent the night with Count Octavian, a 17-year-old who is little more than half her age. As they are breakfasting a visitor is heard arriving and the Princess, believing this to be her husband, hastily instructs Octavian to hide. However it is not her husband, but her coarse country cousin, the Baron Ochs, who interrupts. He has come to ask for the Princess's help in finding a young knight to fulfil the tradition of delivering a silver rose to his new fiancée; she is the 15-year-old Sophie, fresh from the convent, whom he hasn't yet met. Knowing now that the visitor is not the Princesses's husband, Octavian reappears, cheekily dressed as her maid.

Ochs' crude and fairly basic descriptions of his own love-making needs and technique amuse both the Princess and Octavian but "she" now has to suffer Ochs' similarly crude attempts to flirt with "her". Exploiting the situation for her own further amusement the Princess instructs her "maid" to fetch the medallion with Octavian's likeness on it and show it to Ochs, creating more embarrassment for the "maid" as "her" resemblance to the portrait is discussed. Ochs departs, leaving the silver rose with the Princess; she assigns Octavian to be the traditional "Knight of the Rose" and dismisses him. Left alone, she moodily reflects that soon enough he'll be leaving her, as she'll be too old. (She's at the ripe old age of 32 !)

When Octavian delivers the silver rose to Sophie and sees how young and beautiful she is he falls for her instantly; the Baron arrives, starts to maul Sophie and not surprisingly rouses her disgust. She swiftly re-appraises her agreement to marry him, comparing him with Octavian to the Baron's considerable disadvantage. Octavian is equally offended by the Baron's behaviour and decides to prevent this marriage.

Returning to his disguise as the Princess's maid, Octavian welcomes the Baron at an assignation arranged in a private room at an inn, which is furnished with all the necessary accoutrements, including a discreetly placed bed. But all the Baron's advances to the "maid" are frustrated by pre-arranged "noises-off"; then Sophie, the Princess, a police commissar, and Uncle Tom Cobbleigh arrive, to the Baron's great embarrassment and he leaves pursued by the innkeeper and others presenting their bills. In a magnificent final trio, Octavian declares himself for Sophie, she takes him, and the Princess comes to terms with her lost youth.

The Abbé Prevost, and Manon Lescaut

Antoine François, L'Abbé Prévost d'Exiles, is famous for only one thing: his story of Manon Lescaut, which is the seventh and final part of a seven-volume work. The novel is entitled *Histoire du Chevalier des Grieux et de Manon Lescaut* and became the basis of operas by Auber, Massenet, and Puccini. It tells the story of the consequences of the passion of a young man, the Chevalier des Grieux, who throws away everything for Manon Lescaut, an attractive young woman whose simple yet wholly innocent aim in life is to become a lady of pleasure; all she wants is a life of luxury and ease and, aided by her brother who effectively acts as her pimp, she'll go with any man who can provide this for her. Being an attractive young woman she, with the aid of her brother, has no problems finding suitable supporters.

As a young man the Abbé was both religious and, given his calling, over-sexed; he twice enlisted in the army and twice resigned to join the Society of Jesus, where he no doubt hoped to find both spiritual and physical salvation but from which he was ultimately dismissed. He joined the Benedictine monks, became ordained but had to leave over problems concerning a woman. He obtained a position in England as a tutor but lost it over one of his many affairs and went to Holland, where he stayed for five years before having to return to England to escape his debts. In London he spent time in prison over forged documents and finally returned to France, where he died after having achieved a reconciliation with his Church. Both he and his seven-volume work would have long ago disappeared from history had it not been for the high quality and resulting level of interest in his story of Manon Lescaut.

In the novel Manon is guided by her brother (in Massenet's opera, her cousin) Lescaut, who is influential in bringing her to the notice of wealthy men. He observes the Chevalier des Grieux cheating at cards and teaches him how to cheat less obviously; in short, he is not a nice character, but probably not a lot worse than his sister. Manon herself is emotionally faithful to des Grieux but physically will give herself to anyone who can provide her with the luxury she craves. To pay for the lifestyle she wants she has only one currency, herself. At one level therefore, she simply sells sex, just as any courtesan would, but the interest in her derives from Prévost's description of the way her character and behaviour are overlaid with a special kind of innocence, combined with romance and, ultimately, tragedy. Operatically, this is a part which, to be wholly true to Prévost's novel, should be performed by a fine singing actress who can bring out these qualities.

"Manon"   Massenet, 1884

At an inn at Amiens Manon meets her cousin Lescaut, who is to accompany her to a convent; she is accosted by a man who wants to take her away, and in her innocence listens to him but is rescued by the return of Lescaut, who lectures her on the dangers of such chance encounters. Des Grieux appears; he also "chats her up" but more successfully, and in spite of the lecture from her cousin she leaves with him for Paris.

Lescaut and his friend de Bretigny, who was also at the inn at Amiens and had admired Manon, call on her; Lescaut keeps des Grieux's attention while de Bretigny describes to Manon the lifestyle he can provide for her if she will leave des Grieux. She cannot resist the offer and agrees to join him. Later learning that the despairing des Grieux intends to enter the Church, she returns to him and they go off, re-united. In an illegal gambling den des Grieux is persuaded by Manon to join a card game with Lescaut and de Bretigny, but he is accused of cheating and he and Manon are both arrested; he is later released but Manon is convicted of prostitution and sentenced to be deported. Des Grieux bribes a guard for permission to talk with her and tries to persuade her to escape with him while the guard is away, but she no longer has any strength and dies in his arms.

"Manon Lescaut"   Puccini, 1894

Manon and des Grieux meet, fall in love, and go off together as before. Lescaut (here her brother, as in Prévost's book) brings his wealthy friend Geronte to her and Manon deserts des Grieux for the luxurious life that Geronte can provide for her as his mistress. Des Grieux reappears, their love is renewed and Manon agrees to leave Geronte and return to des Grieux, but she is reluctant to leave behind all her beautiful jewels and Geronte appears as she is selecting from them. He calls the police and, accused of theft and prostitution, Manon is sentenced to be deported to the New World. Failing in a rescue attempt at Le Havre, des Grieux persuades the captain to allow him to board and travel with her.

In America des Grieux and Manon have escaped and are wandering in the desert beyond New Orleans; she is exhausted and faints. Des Grieux leaves her to search for water but returns unsuccessful; finally Manon, singing of her love for him, dies of exhaustion.

EPILOGUE: WOMEN IN OPERA

Opera heroines in serious (as distinct from comic) opera tend to get a poor deal; if they're not the natural victims of men they go mad, or die from consumption, or commit suicide. Not always, of course, because there are quite a few operas in which they survive; there are even operas where there is a "real" heroine (in the sense of actually *doing* something rather than just surviving various physical and/or emotional ordeals); and sometimes she even rescues the hero (i.e. the tenor) from whatever might have been his fate, and provides a happier one for him in her arms. Nevertheless, the great majority of opera's leading ladies do seem to expire at the end.

In the old Greek myths there are no heroines; in the literal sense of the word all the "heroic" acts are performed by men, the heroes; never by women. These women are never more than Leading Ladies and some, like Medea, Circe, are villainesses rather than virtuous ladies. The women of these mythic stories are the (usually) passive objects of male lust who get raped (Cassandra), or submit to seduction (Helen), or play mere supporting roles to their men. Only occasionally in these myths does a woman get to *do* something, like Medea or Clytemnestra, or Alceste; even Electra, who really intended to kill her mother, actually left the job to her brother. It's an approach that is carried through into opera.

Opera's leading ladies, who are usually described as heroines even if they aren't *literally* so, don't often have the opportunity to be in control, to be the "doers" rather than the "done by". *Turandot,* the leading lady (not, I think, the heroine) of Puccini's opera, is one such; taking her revenge for the betrayal centuries earlier of a princess by a man, she has developed a plan that exploits her beauty to lead men to their deaths. Lady Macbeth is another; it's her husband who kills the king, but she's the power behind his dagger. And there are opera women drawn from history, who have demonstrably been in control (the Queens Elizabeth, Semiramide, Dido). But these tend to be the exceptions. Women are usually portrayed by the librettists as weak-natured or just plain romantically silly types, to the point where, in Verdi's *Rigoletto* for example, it seems to me that Gilda is characterised as just a simpleton. Yet even when a woman is given a strong character she usually comes to a sticky end (Semiramide, Dido, Cassandra, Salome, Brünnhilde, Tosca, for example). If someone wanted to make a case for a politically-correct revisionist treatment of opera, there's some useful ammunition here.

Sex in opera doesn't have to have seduction as a preliminary; in fact more usually seduction doesn't come into it at all. *He* wants *her*, she definitely doesn't want him, so to have her requires either a brutal rape (as of *Lucretia*), or perhaps just a simple exercise of authority; as for example in the often found guardian/ward relationship. He (the guardian) simply tells her (the ward) that they are to be married, the real point of which is just to obtain her sexual services. Just as often, marriage is not on offer; he just wants her and uses blackmail and threats to achieve his ends. In these operas the underlying sexual tension introduced in this way is but one thread or sub-plot of a number in the whole work, and a great deal of additional colour is given to the working out of the opera by the manner in which the girl responds to the pressure being exerted on her.

Thus Leonora, in Verdi's *Il Trovatore*, offers herself as a bribe to the Count di Luna in a desperate attempt to save the life of the man she loves, and then takes poison rather than be dishonoured, as she sees it, by honouring that promise. Whereas Puccini's *Tosca* on the other hand, having been told that if she doesn't submit to Scarpia's virtual rape he'll kill her lover, secures the promise of Cavaradossi's release and their freedom and then finds an opportunity to kill Scarpia. These are not just two different heroines, they are two women of completely different calibre who react in different ways to their situations. A variation on this theme is to introduce a third man, as in Verdi's *Ernani*; da Silva, Elvira's elderly uncle and guardian, intends to marry her, but she detests him and loves Ernani, the bandit; the King enters and tells Elvira that he too loves her, but she spurns him; his knowledge of her love for Ernani arouses his jealousy and makes him try to abduct her.

There is however one discernible divide in the operatic treatments of women. As a general rule, in serious opera they get the rough end of whatever deal is going, whereas in *comic* opera they nearly always achieve what they want, with the implied conclusion that soprano and tenor live together happily ever after. Could that be why it's *comic* opera?

Mad women

There seemed to be a brief period in the 19th century when it appeared that an opera might not succeed if there wasn't a mad scene. The heroine had to break down under pressure (*Lucia di Lammermoor*), or buckle under the shock of apparent desertion by her betrothed (*I Puritani*), or just be unable to handle the situation when the beloved breaks off the engagement (*La Sonnambula*).

Lucia di Lammermoor is a nice girl, of fragile mental health in the first place, from a decent Scottish family, who loves the wrong man (i.e. not the one whom her overbearing brother wants her to marry). Nevertheless she "weds" him by a simple declaration to each other that they are married in the sight of heaven; however, because he must leave Scotland immediately there is no opportunity (nor seemingly any desire) to consummate the union. Lucia's brother is determined that she will marry the man whose money will save the family estates; he tricks and bullies her into the marriage by convincing her that her absent lover has forgotten her. But no sooner has she signed the marriage contract (in spite of her earlier vows) than he appears, to claim her as his own. But she has to go with her new husband to the marital bedroom. And when she later appears in a blood-stained night-gown, it's his blood all over it, not hers; she'd cracked under the pressure of events and the shock of seeing her beloved, killed her bridegroom and then totally lost her marbles. But her "mad scene" is absolutely the finest of its kind and *the* highlight of the opera. Lucia, it seems to me, is not a woman one can identify with, or even empathise with; she's just too weak-minded, and it seems no loss when she subsequently dies of a nervous breakdown.

I Puritani Set in England during the time of Oliver Cromwell's Commonwealth, this tells of Elvira, the daughter of a Puritan family, who loves the Cavalier Arturo and is allowed by her father to marry him. After the betrothal party Arturo learns that Queen Henrietta, the widow of the executed King Charles, is a prisoner in the castle and is to be taken to London for almost certain execution. The quick-witted Cavalier spots an opportunity to smuggle her out of the castle; he quickly borrows Elvira's bridal headdress as a "cover" for her, they manage to leave the castle and he escorts her to France. Yet in spite of having just been formally betrothed to him Elvira, not knowing about Queen Henrietta, can only believe that Arturo has abandoned her to run off with another woman. The shock of this apparent betrayal sends her mad, but when some time later Arturo returns and is able to rejoin her (after one or two dramas) this second shock restores her sanity. What is to be said about such a girl? That her love wasn't strong enough to sustain her through a difficult period? She's too superficial to be worth anyone's time, least of all that of a red-blooded Cavalier who would surely have been better off to have remained in France and found a passionate mademoiselle rather than risk his life returning for one such as Elvira. Both of these operas derive from novels by Sir Walter Scott, but *his* heroines had a bit more backbone than their operatic counterparts. But at least Elvira survived to live happily ever after with her Cavalier.

La Sonnambula is Bellini's opera about a girl who, unknown to herself or anyone else, is in the habit of walking in her sleep; one night she sleep-walks into the bedroom of a local lord and leaves evidence of her visit. Her fiancé can't handle the inferences of this and demands his ring back, whereupon she goes mad with grief. Eventually the whole village, including her ex-fiancé, observe her somnambulism; he makes a handsome apology and returns her ring, whereupon her sanity is restored. This girl is like Elvira; emotional shocks go straight to the brain and upset her balance; what she should have done was to have refused to accept his ring or his apology, and made him grovel. However, like Elvira she too lived happily ever after, (one presumes), with her fiancé.

Macbeth's wife, Lady Macbeth, didn't go mad in the sense that the three previous ladies did but she certainly seemed to be suffering from quite serious delusional problems, highlighted in her famous sleep-walking scene. In the opera her death is reported to Macbeth in the very next scene, and since she had previously come across as much the stronger of the two of them, it seems very likely that her condition took a very sudden turn for the worse. Perhaps she didn't die from madness, but there's a case for it.

'Die for love' women

Rigoletto's daughter Gilda is, in character terms, one of the least credible women in opera. Her character is so weak that it must surely bring discredit on the whole female sex. Having been kept in virtual purdah by her father, seeing only him and her maid, she is understandably quite easily wooed by the handsome, libertine Duke when he discovers her; reasonably enough, she can have no idea that she is just the newest target of a serial seducer. But when later she is kidnapped by the Duke's men, carried off to his palace for his pleasure and there seduced (raped?) by him, one would think she would at least understand that he was not the sort of person she should get to know any better. And when her father later takes her to watch the Duke romancing another woman she still can't really feel badly about him. Worse, learning of the plot to assassinate the Duke, she submits herself in male disguise as the alternative victim, quite deliberately and voluntarily sacrificing her life to save his. A complete innocent who had been courted and then (quite probably) raped by the man who had so expertly wooed her, she still wants to die for him. Opera doesn't need much verismo but this is surely way over the top in the unreality of its heroine. Gilda must surely be the silliest woman in all opera.

Dido and Aeneas however does have a real woman in Queen Dido. This is truly a noble and courageous woman who dies for real adult love, not some kind of adolescent infatuation. Having fled from her murderous brother, she led her court almost to the other side of the known world and there established the new city of Carthage and a new realm under her rule. After her dead husband, the only man she finds worthy of her is Aeneas, the last surviving Prince of Troy, and she falls for him in a big way. Then when his destiny calls him away from her, and neither her pleadings nor her curses can hold him, she decides to cleanse him from her memory by burning everything that reminds her of him; only to realise that she does not want to live without him and decides that she too will perish in the pyre.

This woman, one feels, would have been worth giving up one's destiny for. Yet in the end, she lies dead whilst Aeneas sails off to found Rome, a task that could well have been left to those other survivors, the twins Romulus and Remus, who got the credit for it anyway.

Norma, Bellini's heroine in the eponymous opera, is cast in the same mould as Dido. Her lover's betrayal of her is more down to earth in that he leaves her for another woman instead of a vision of destiny, but Norma's reaction is equally vigorous. As the Druid High-Priestess she is accustomed to authority and decision-making, and when her faithless lover Pollione is captured and brought to her, her aria "In mia man" is a triumph of menace and threat (particularly as sung by Maria Callas). Nevertheless, he must die, and she resolves to die with him since then she will be with him forever. Pollione, too late, realises that she is a woman worth living for, though he would have done better for them both by staying faithful to her.

Wagner's **Tristan und Isolde** has a very tragic heroine in Isolde. Tristan had previously killed her fiancé, yet somehow she couldn't bring herself to kill him in revenge when she had the opportunity. Now, on the ship from Ireland, he is ferrying her to a loveless marriage with his uncle the King of Cornwall, but all she wants is to die. The fates however are against her, for a poison she and Tristan have just taken (he having taken it with her in an act of atonement) turns out to be a love potion substituted by her maid Brangäne, and she and Tristan fall deeply in love. In despair at the turn of events, she faints. In Cornwall, they fall into the trap of a clandestine assignation, are betrayed, curse their love, and pray for death; Tristan soon gets his wish when, as he kisses Isolde, he allows himself to be severely wounded by their betrayer. He is taken to his own castle in Brittany to recover and await Isolde's coming, but almost as soon as she arrives, he dies in her arms. Her husband the King arrives, to the accompaniment of a certain amount of mayhem; he's chased after her to say that he's heard from Brangäne about the love potion and forgives her; but Isolde has a vision of Tristan's new life in everlasting death, and dies, transfigured.

Aida, Verdi's captive Ethiopian princess, also prefers to die rather than live without the man she loves. Having already been prepared to betray her countrymen for the sake of the noble Egyptian Radames, she finds a way into the place where he is to be entombed alive, so that she can die with him. Aside from her love for Radames she has every justification for this course, since otherwise she would remain as the personal slave of the jealous and frustrated Princess Amneris, who could not be expected to provide her with a reasonable lifestyle. At least her unhappy time in slavery can be redeemed by a few final hours of bliss in the arms of the man she loves. Hers, I feel, is a worthy way out, made more so by the fact that in this case it is the hero, Radames, who is supposed to be the only one to die.

Woman as victim

Otello's wife Desdemona, in Verdi's opera, is the innocent pawn in Iago's scheme to bring about Otello's downfall. Maddened by his totally unreasoning jealousy, Otello kills his loving faithful wife who hasn't sinned against anyone. It's a great part in an even greater opera, but it doesn't do anything for Desdemona.

La Forza del Destino has yet another one of Verdi's unfortunates, and it's another Leonora. Because of her love and respect for her father, who won't let her marry Don Alvaro, she dithers over their elopement, allowing her father to discover them; in the ensuing brawl, Alvaro accidentally kills her father. They flee in different directions, with Leonora's brother Don Carlo vowing to find and kill them both. In the final act he has met Alvaro again, goaded him into a duel and been fatally wounded; as he lies dying his sister, now a hermit, finds him and tries to tend to his wounds. Carlo recognises her and with his final breath he curses her for the dishonour she has brought to the family, and then fatally stabs her. And all because she couldn't make up her mind at the beginning of the opera. As that great 20th-century feminist Mae West noted: "(S)he who hesitates...is a damned fool".

Bizet's **Carmen** is possibly the best known of all the tragic heroines of opera, in her case as the victim of a weak man who'd briefly been the focus of her free-spirited love. Her mistake was to believe that her "love em and leave em" style was appropriate for all her male fancies, that just because she'd warned each man of what she was like, he'd go off quietly when his time was up. José has thrown away too much in his infatuation for her, and this wonderfully attractive free spirit is killed by her rejected lover just outside the bullring where the toreador, her latest one, is doing his thing. A marvellous heroine of a hugely popular opera, but one who at the end lies just as dead as all the other heroines.

Survivor women

that is, those who are still alive at the end of the opera, with or without their heroes; there aren't many, but they do exist.

Werther , by Massenet, has Charlotte as the girl who marries the wrong man, Albert, because this was her dying mother's wish, even though she is aware of having strong feelings for Werther. Deprived of his one true love, Werther makes an excuse to borrow Albert's pistols and uses them to commit suicide, surviving only long enough for the obligatory final duet with Charlotte. The ending is in the *Traviata/Bohème* tradition but with an interesting reversal of roles.

Fidelio, otherwise known as Leonore, the eponymous heroine of Beethoven's opera is another; disguised as a man, she has taken a job in the gaol where her husband Florestan is incarcerated as a political prisoner, hoping to find and release him. She achieves this in the nick of time, just before he is to be secretly disposed of. The Minister arrives as she is holding-off the would-be assassin at gunpoint, he frees Florestan and the other political prisoners, and arrests the villain; everyone joins in a chorus of praise to the brave woman who saved her husband. This is an unusual happy ending, with both heroine and hero surviving to enjoy their mutual love.

La fanciulla del West (Puccini's "The girl of the Golden West") is another. Minnie --- the "girl" of the title --- is adored by the miners in the township where she runs the local bar, and is loved by the Sheriff, but she doesn't return his love; she's still looking for the right man. This turns out to be the outlaw Ramerrez, whom the Sheriff is hunting. He appears in Minnie's bar as "Johnson" and he and Minnie soon discover a mutual attraction. The Sheriff discovers Johnson hiding in Minnie's cabin; she pleads for him and suggests a game of poker; if the Sheriff wins Minnie will marry him; if she wins, the Sheriff lets Johnson go. She wins, but only by cheating in the final hand, and Johnson is free, to return to the only life he knows. Later comes news that he has been captured by the miners, and is to be hanged from a nearby tree; Minnie arrives in time to plead for his life, and the miners give way to her because of all she's done for them. She leaves with Johnson, to make a new life with him.

Rape: or 'Death rather than Dishonour'.

The Rape of Lucretia, Benjamin Britten's operatic version of Shakespeare's poem, is an example of a man taking by force what he cannot have any other way, and of the woman's reaction. Roman generals had been discussing the fidelity of their wives and discovered that only Collatinus' wife Lucretia was chaste, all the others having been discovered by their husbands *in flagrante delicto.*

One of these generals was Sextus Tarquinius, son of Tarquinius Superbus ("the proud"), hated Prince of Rome; Sextus felt that for Lucretia to be the only chaste wife in Rome was not good for his future political rivalry with Collatinus, and secretly left the camp at night for Rome, where he called on Lucretia and was provided with accommodation. He later entered her bedroom, raped her and rode back to the camp. Lucretia sent for her husband and her father, told them what happened, and demanded vows of revenge from them. Their fulfilment of these vows led to the overthrow of the House of Tarquinius but Lucretia was not around to see it. A good, sinless and innocent patrician Roman matron, she nevertheless preferred to die rather than live with the knowledge of what was done to her and, having extracted the promises from her husband and father she fell on her husband's sword. She chose death *because of* not *rather than* dishonour, but her end was the same.

Tosca, in Puccini's eponymous opera, is the greatest of the women forced into a rape scenario. Beautiful, talented, emotional, capable of jealousy even of a woman in a portrait, she is an independent, strong-willed actress and singer, with a life and a lover of her own. The feared police chief Scarpia wants her and finds an opportunity to compel her submission. As he moves triumphantly to take his first preliminary kiss she grasps a knife from his dinner table, stabs him in the back as he embraces her, and while he lies dying on the floor mocks him about the taste of her kisses. In spite of this triumph however she cannot escape his treachery and is forced to commit suicide by jumping from the top of the Castle.

Il Trovatore ("The Troubadour") is Manrico, the bandit who loves and is loved by (yet another) Leonora, in Verdi's opera of this title. She is also desired by the Count di Luna, whom she definitely doesn't want. Manrico falls into the clutches of his rival and is to be executed but Leonora buys his life by promising herself to the Count. Before going to Manrico to tell him that he can escape, she takes poison to avoid the fate she has provided for herself. Manrico's code of honour won't allow him to escape on the basis of her deal, though he learns too late about the poison; she dies and he is executed anyway, thus completely nullifying her sacrifice. In this opera there's a second lady, the gypsy Azucena who is central to the story; when the opera ends she too is about to be led out to her execution. There's no long-term future for women in serious opera.

Comedy heroines

"Comedy" rather than "comic" because in context it's more accurate; and anyway it applies to the opera itself, not to the heroine, who's often a girl of spirit and intelligence; usually one of her protagonists is the "comic" character, a buffoon who can't see through the wool she's pulled over his eyes.

Spirited fillies

Rosina in Rossini's *Barber of Seville* (who re-appears as the Countess in Mozart's *Marriage of Figaro*) is one such; her scheming with Figaro (the Barber) to avoid having to marry her guardian Dr.Bartolo is the essence of this ever-popular work, and at the end she gets her man (Count Almaviva), and his money, though she loved him anyway even when she thought he was just a poor student.

Donizetti provided a very entertaining heroine, Norina, in **Don Pasquale**. Pasquale is planning to re-marry and to disinherit his nephew Ernesto, who is Norina's fiancé; to thwart this plan Norina "marries" Pasquale herself. The moment the marriage "contract" is signed she transforms herself from the appealing, only-just-out-of-the-convent, desperately shy virginal girl whom Pasquale thought he was getting, into a spendthrift spitfire who puts the fear of God into him. All is later revealed to him, he's permanently put off any further marriage plans, and Norina's future with Ernesto is assured, both romantically and financially.

The fairy tale winner

Another happy winner of both man and money is the lovely Cinderella; Rossini's **La Cenerentola** contains all the principal elements of the fairy tale, which is too well-known to bear repetition here. For Cinderella, even her ugly sisters have redeeming qualities, and for one so pure in heart and mind, no reward is too great.

Little rich girl

Another of Donizetti's comic operas is **L'Elisir d'Amore** ("The Elixir of Love"). Here the conventional financial and social positions are reversed. The wealthy heroine Adina is far more worldly, though that's a relative term in this opera of country rustics, than her swain, the simple peasant Nemorino, whose love she gently refuses. To his dismay, not only does she refuse him but she is apparently swept off her feet by the flashy gallant, Sergeant of the army Belcore, planning to marry him that very evening. In despair, the desperately poor Nemorino goes to Belcore and accepts the "King's Shilling" as his fee for enlisting; thus he will have enough money to buy a magical elixir from the itinerant quack Dr. Dulcamara, an elixir which will guarantee that all the girls (including Adina) will fall in love with him.

Nemorino is unaware of news reaching the village that his uncle has just died and left him a lot of money, and so attributes his sudden popularity with the girls to the effectiveness of the elixir. Adina is put out by his apparent sudden indifference to her (he is simply waiting for the elixir to work its magic on her too) and, refusing a bottle of Dulcamara's elixir for herself, declares she will win him back with her feminine charms alone. Having heard from Belcore that Nemorino has signed up, she buys back his enlistment; Nemorino, seeing her with a tear on her face, sings "Una furtiva lagrima", the best aria in the whole very tuneful work, expressing hope that there may yet be hope for him. But when they are together he still affects indifference, compelling her to admit that she bought back his papers out of love for him. Everything ends happily, and even Dr. Dulcamara comes to wonder whether perhaps his Bordeaux wine "elixir" does have magical properties after all. Since Adina, like Nemorino himself, didn't know the news about his uncle we can be sure she really was declaring her love for the young man she had always known, although it's now turned to out be a much more suitable match.

Daddy's girl

From his *Il Trittico* group of three one-act operas, Puccini's comedy **Gianni Schicchi**, almost a black comedy, is possibly the most amusing of all the comic operas. The setting is Florence in the year 1299, and we are in the bedroom of the late wealthy merchant Buoso Donati, who has only just died; in fact he still lies on his deathbed as his relatives discuss his will, and in particular the rumour that he has left everything to the monks. But if they could only find his will, then just maybe they could do something about it before it is published...

Rinuccio, one of the younger relatives, loves Lauretta, daughter of the shrewd peasant Gianni Schicchi, and gets his aunt's permission to marry her if they can find the will and all turns out well for the family ("yes, then you can marry whom you like, even the devil's daughter"). There's a hunt for it, and meantime Rinuccio secretly sends for Schicchi and Lauretta. The will is found, and the rumours are proved true; everything goes to the monks. Gianni arrives with Lauretta. In their disappointment, Rinuccio's family now refuse him permission to marry the daughter of such a low-born peasant, especially since she has no dowry, and tell Schicchi to leave and take his daughter with him. Gianni's pride initially makes him refuse to help Lauretta in this situation, but her appeal to him, in the opera's best known number, *"O mio babbino caro"* ("O my beloved daddy"), that she cannot live without Rinuccio, wins him round.

He instructs the family to move the body to another room, and to send for the notary. He takes the place of the dead man, now only close to death, and, having warned the family of the risks they all run if their scheme is discovered, explains that he's going to dictate a new will to the notary. Approving such a clever idea, the family agree that they must leave the distribution of assets to him, each one bribing him to look after his or her own interests. With the notary now present and taking down "Buoso's" instructions, he leaves various small items to each family member and then, coming to the really valuable ones, including the house, leaves all of these to "my dear, devoted, affectionate friend Gianni Schicchi". The relatives are furious, but helpless; Schicchi chases them all out of what is now his house, while Rinuccio and Lauretta are seen on the balcony in each other's arms. True to form, the penniless girl ends up happily with her man and his (or now her father's) money.

....and finally, Woman on top

Pergolesi's *La Serva Padrona* ("The maidservant turned mistress") --- see also the introduction to Chapter 10 --- tells how Uberto's life and household are run, to his complete dissatisfaction, by his housekeeper Serpina; and how, when he attempts to assert his authority, he is no match for her in argument. In desperation he instructs his mute servant Vespone (these three are the entire cast, and one of them never makes a sound) to go and find him a wife. "Great idea" says Serpina, "And I'm the ideal woman!" She sets out, in their duet, the points in her favour, while Uberto fears that, as usual, this is another argument he's going to lose.

Serpina decides she'll have to trick her master into the marriage and sets up a scheme with Vespone. He will be introduced as Captain Tempest, a soldier who is going to marry Serpina; but the "Captain", an ill-tempered man, demands, through Serpina, that her master provides her with a dowry or marries her himself. For Uberto, it's clearly better that he marries the woman himself. With this settled the "Captain" reveals himself as Vespone, and Uberto's protests gradually disappear as he comes to realise that he loves Serpina after all, and will marry her.

This is a case of "winner takes all", and Serpina is the clear winner; she still runs the house, she's about to become her master's wife and equal, and quite soon, if the past is anything to go by, he'll be her servant!